A Straightforward Guide
To
Pensions and the Pensions Industry
Patrick Grant

Straightforward Guides

ISBN

978-1-84716-900-6

Printed by 4edge www.4edge.co.uk

Editor: Roger Sproston

Cover design by Straightforward Graphics

Whilst every effort has been made to ensure that the information contained within this book is correct at the time of going to press, the author and publisher can take no responsibility for the errors or omissions contained within.

Wolverhampton City Council	
X400 000005 6797	
Askews & Holts	03-Jun-2019
	£9.99
	1CL

Contents

Introduction

Chapter 1-Pensions and Planning for the Future   11
Planning for the future   11
Sources of pension and other retirement income   11
The Pensioners Income Series   12
Average income of pensioners-couples   12
Average income of pensioners-Singles   13
Regional incomes   15

Chapter 2-Income needed in Retirement   21
-Planning Ahead
Income needs in retirement   21
What period to save over   22
Inflation   22
Everyday needs   24
The impact of inflation   26

Chapter 3-Sources of Pensions-A Summary   29
The State Pension   29
The over 80 pension   30
Occupational pensions   30
Stakeholder schemes   31
How much can be invested in a stakeholder pension?   32
Other ways to save for retirement   33

Chapter 4-The State Pension   35
Who is entitled?   35
Transexuals   36
How many qualifying years to get the full State Pension?   37
Using someone else's contribution record   37

Class 1 contributions   39
Class 2 contributions   39
Class 3 contributions   39
Class 4 Contributions   39
Pension credits   40
The guarantee credit   40
The savings credit   40
If you reach State Pension age on or after 6 April 2016   42
National Insurance Credits   42
The State Pension age   43
Additional state pension   44
Contracting out   45
Increasing your state pension   45
Filling gaps in your record   45
Deferring your state pension   47
Women and Pensions   53
Particular issues for women   53
Effects of changes to the state pension on women   55
Have you told the government you are a carer?   55

Chapter 5-Private Pension Savings-General   **57**
The lifetime allowance   57
Protecting the Lifetime Allowance   58
The annual allowance   60
Limits to benefits and contributions   60
Taking a pension   61

Chapter 6-Choosing a Personal Pension Plan   **65**
Investments   65
Self-invested Personal Pensions (SIPPs)   65
How it works   66
What you can and can't invest in   66

How you access money in your SIPP   67
Small Self-Administered Schemes (Ssas)   67
Releasing funds to finance business   69
Fees and other charges   70
Other benefits from a personal pension   70
Retirement due to ill-health   71
The Pension Protection Fund   72
The Financial Assistance Scheme   72
In the case of fraud or theft   73
The Pension Tracing Service   73

Chapter 7-Job Related (Occupational) Pensions   75
Limits on your pension savings   75
Tax advantages of occupational schemes   76
Qualifying to join an occupational scheme   78
Automatic enrolment   78
Choosing a pension scheme   81
Pension entitlements   82
Final salary schemes   82
Money purchase schemes   83
The cash balance scheme   84
Tax   85
Contributions into occupational schemes   85
Contracting Out Through Occupational Schemes   87
Rules-defined benefit pension scheme   87

Chapter 8-Group Personal Pension Schemes   89
What is a group personal pension?   89
How your pension grows while you are working   89
What you need to think about   91
Changing jobs   91

Chapter 9-Stakeholder Pensions   **93**
About stakeholder pensions   93
Stakeholder pensions defined   93
Who should take out a stakeholder pension?   95
How much can be invested in a stakeholder pension?   95
Trust schemes and non-trust schemes   96
Financial Conduct Authority (FCA)   96
Financial advice on stakeholder pensions   96
Tax and national insurance   97
Tax relief   97
Regular information for members   97
Existing employer stakeholder schemes   98
Automatic enrolment and stakeholder pensions   98
Contributions to stakeholder pension employer schemes   98
Monitoring by scheme managers or trustees   99

Chapter 10-Leaving an Occupational Scheme   **101**
Obtaining a refund of contributions   101

Chapter 11-Transferring Pension Rights   **103**
Transferring your pension   103
UK Transfers   104
Overseas transfers   104
Things to think about   108
Moving abroad   110
Building up a state pension from abroad   113
Receive a UK state pension abroad   113

Chapter 12-Pensions for the Self-Employed   **115**
The State Pension   116
How best to save for retirement   116
Make the most of your pension pot   116

Self-employed: what kind of pension should I use? 117
What is the annual allowance? 118
Rules for doctors and dentists 118

Chapter 13-Pensions and Benefits for Dependants **121**
State pensions 121
Death after retirement 122
Occupational and personal schemes 122
Dependant's pensions from occupational schemes 123
Lump sum death benefits 123

Chapter 14-Protecting Pensions **125**
Occupational schemes 126
Other schemes 128
Protection of personal pensions 129
Complaining about pensions-State pensions 129
Occupational pensions 130
Personal pensions 130

Chapter 15 Options for Retirement and Tax **131**
Retirement options and taxation of pensions 131
Options for using your pension pot 131
Keep your pension savings where they are 132
Use your pension pot to get a guaranteed income for life 134
The options 134
Basic lifetime annuities 134
Investment-linked annuities 135
Tax issues 137
Use your pot to provide a flexible retirement income 138
Tax issues 140
Take your pension pot as a number of lump sums 141
Tax issues 143

Take your pension pot in one go   144
Tax issues   145
Mixing your options   145
Tax-free lump sums when mixing options   146

Chapter 16-Reaching Retirement Age   **147**
How to claim state pension   148
How the pension is paid   148
Leaving the country   148
Pensions from an occupational scheme   149
A pension from a personal plan   150
New regulations for pension providers   151
Advice schemes for pensions   151
Beware of scams   152
The Pensions Dashboard   153
Inheriting pensions on death   153

Useful addresses
Index

****

Introduction

The subject of pensions and the provision of pensions has been a hotly debated topic over the last decade. Essentially, the issue of catering for future needs has been a problem that has vexed government, employers and individuals.

This book takes a look at the issues surrounding pensions and also discusses the different areas of provision, from the state pension to personal pensions and also the tax and benefits implications. We also take a look at accessing pension funds to boost business, which is not widely known or understood.

One thing is for sure, if a person does not, either through an occupational scheme or through some other type of personal pension plan, ensure that they are saving regularly to provide a decent level of pension for their retirement, then they will find themselves, as millions have, in a poverty trap, relying on the state pension alone.

The government is currently reviewing what should happen to the State Pension Age after 2028. This is because people are living longer, which means that pensions are becoming increasingly expensive to provide. Ultimately, there will be pressure to reduce the overall bill, and to gradually increase the retirement age.

All too often, people wake up to the need to build up a pension fund when it is too late. When a person is young, the last thing they want to be thinking about is saving for their old age.

The whole thrust of this book is to help individuals understand the pensions system in the United Kingdom, to open eyes to the implications of not providing for retirement and to point the way to the right sort of plan for them.

The book is split into 4 different sections, the first section covering planning for pensions and pensions generally, the second section covering sources of pensions, state pension, occupational pensions, stakeholder pensions and other forms of savings. The third section covers pensions for dependants and also pensions for self employed and for professionals such as doctors and dentists. Protection of pensions is also covered. Finally, we discuss options for taking your pension and the tax implications of doing so.

One such option which is outlined is that of using your pension pot to fund your business, which can be done before you reach the age of 55. At the very least, the information contained within should enable a person to make an informed choice and to begin to provide security for the future.

This book relates to pensions generally but recognises that the systems and rates are different in Scotland. For more information concerning Scotland go to: www.citizensadvice.org.uk/scotland/debt-and-money/pensions

Finally, please note that at the time of writing the pension and associated figures available relate to the tax year 2018/2019. For the current 2019/2020 figures readers should go to the HMRC website https://www.gov.uk/contact-hmrc or www.pensionsadvisoryservice.org.uk

Patrick Grant 2019

****

Chapter 1

Pensions and Planning for the Future

Planning for the future

The main principle with all pension provision is that the sooner you start saving money in a pension plan the more you will have at retirement. The later that you leave it the less you will have or the more expensive that it will be to create a fund adequate enough for your needs.

In order to gauge your retirement needs, you will need to have a clear idea of your lifestyle, or potential lifestyle in retirement. This is not something that you can plan, or want to plan, at a younger age but the main factor is that the more that you have the easier life will be. There are two main factors which currently underpin retirement:

- Improved health and longevity-we are living longer and we have better health so therefore we are more active
- People are better off-improved state and company pensions

Sources of pension and other retirement income

Government statistics indicate that there is a huge gap between the poorest and richest pensioners in the United Kingdom. No surprise there. The difference between the richest fifth of single pensioners and the poorest fifth is about £400 per week. The poorest fifth of pensioners in the UK are reliant mainly on state benefits whilst the wealthier groups have occupational incomes and also personal investment incomes. The outline below indicates sources of pension and also the disparity between the richest and poorest socio-economic groups:

The Pensioners Income Series

The Pensioners' Incomes (PI) Series, produced by the Government, contains estimates of the levels, sources and distribution of pensioners' incomes. It also examines the position of pensioners within the income distribution of the population as a whole.

Pensioners Income Series 2016/2017

Pensioners have seen an increase in their average weekly incomes over the past decade

- After the deduction of direct taxes, other payments such as pension contributions and housing costs, the average income of all pensioners in 2016/17 was £307 per week. This is a statistically significant increase from 2006/07 when it was £260. This change reflects increases in occupational pension, earnings and benefits.
- In 2016/17 the average income for pensioner couples was £452 per week. This was more than twice that of single pensioners, who had an average income of £214 per week. This difference is statistically significant.
- Income flattened slightly around 2009/10 after the financial crisis which began in 2008.

One fifth of pensioner couples' income was from earnings

- Pensioners receive income from a range of different sources and changes in the composition of these sources reflect important underlying economic factors.

- In 2016/17, benefit income was the largest component of total gross income for pensioner couples and single pensioners. This percentage was 56 per cent for single pensioners, for pensioner couples this was 36 per cent.
- Income from occupational pension was 31 per cent of total gross income for pensioner couples and 28 per cent for single pensioners.
- Income from earnings made up seven per cent of total income for single pensioners. For pensioner couples, one fifth of total income was from earnings. A pensioner couple can sometimes include one adult below SPa who may be working.
- Pensioner couples where one is over SPa and one is under had a weekly average income from earnings of £439. Average income from earnings was £291 per week for pensioner couples where they were both over SPa.

Older pensioners had lower incomes than younger pensioners

- Both recently retired pensioners and pensioners where the head was under 75 had higher average incomes than those where the head was 75 or over. These results were statistically significant.
- In 2016/17, their average incomes were £380, £361 and £265 per week, respectively. Recently retired pensioners are also included in the 'Under 75' age group.
- In 2016/17 the majority of pensioners where the head is 75 or over were single pensioners (64 per cent). On average single pensioners have lower incomes. More information about single pensioners' incomes is discussed on the previous page.

Almost one third of the total income for pensioners was from occupational pensions

- Earnings accounted for 22 per cent of total gross income for recently retired pensioners and pensioners where the head was under 75. For pensioners where the head was aged 75 or over, this was four per cent. Older pensioners are less likely to be in work and hence receive a smaller amount from earnings.

- Benefit income made up more than half of total gross income for pensioners where the head was aged 75 or over. For recently retired pensioners and pensioners where the head was under 75, benefit income made up 34 per cent and 36 per cent of total gross income respectively.

- Occupational pension income was 29 per cent of total gross income for recently retired pensioners and pensioners where the head was under 75. This was 31 per cent for pensioners where the head was aged 75 or over.

- Incomes from personal pension and investment were similar percentages of total gross income for all groups.

- In 2016/17 53 per cent of recently retired pensioners received more than 50 per cent of their gross income from private sources.

Single men had a higher income than single women

- Single male pensioners had higher average incomes than single female pensioners. In 2016/17, single men had an average weekly income of £233 and single women had an average weekly income of £206. This difference is statistically significant.

- The difference was greatest among pensioners aged over 75. Single men in this age group had an average weekly income of £246 per week compared to women who had an

average weekly income of £204 per week. This difference is statistically significant.
- In 2016/17 the majority of single female pensioners were aged 75 and over (58 per cent). As seen on page four, older pensioners on average have lower incomes.

Over half of the total income for single women pensioners was from benefit income
- The difference in incomes reflects differences in the components that make up an individual's total gross income.
- Benefit income made up 61 per cent of total gross income for single women. For single men, this value was 48 per cent.
- Thirty-one per cent of total gross income for single men was from occupational pension. For single women, this was 26 per cent.
- Income from earnings made up nine per cent of total gross income for single men. For single women, this was six per cent.

Regional differences
Pensioner incomes differed between regions and countries.
When looking at regional incomes we take the average weekly income (AHC) for each region over the three year period 2014/15 to 2016/17, adjusted to 2016/17 prices.
- For pensioner couples, the majority of regions have average weekly incomes below the UK average.
- The UK average weekly income over this three year period was £447 for pensioner couples.
- On average, pensioner couple incomes were lowest in

Wales, where income was 12 per cent below the UK average. In comparison, pensioner couples in the South East had the highest average incomes, 12 per cent higher than the UK average. This difference is statistically significant.

■ Pensioner couples in Scotland average income was the same as the UK average.

Sources of pensioner incomes -Percentage of pensioners receiving income from private pensions has increased

■ Nearly all pensioners (97 per cent) were in receipt of the State Pension in 2016/17. This has increased from 1996/97, where 94 per cent of all pensioners were in receipt of State Pension. This result is statistically significant.

■ Income-related benefits were received by 24 per cent of all pensioners in 2016/17. The percentage of pensioners in receipt has decreased from 37 per cent in 1996/97; this is statistically significant. This reflects for example increases in other sources of income, particularly income from State Pension and Private Pension, reducing eligibility to Income related benefits for pensioners.

■ Twenty-one per cent of pensioners were in receipt of disability benefits in 2016/17; this has increased by three percentage points from 1996/97. This increase is statistically significant.

■ Over the past 20 years, there has been an increase of nine percentage points in the percentage of pensioners receiving income from private pensions – from 62 per cent to 71 per cent; this is statistically significant.

■ There has been an increase of three percentage points in the percentage of pensioners with income from occupational pensions – from 59 per cent in 1996/97 to 62 per cent in 2016/17.

- Personal pensions provide income to a smaller group of pensioners than occupational pensions. In 2016/17, 19 per cent of pensioners were in receipt of income from personal pensions, compared with four per cent in 1996/97. This increase is statistically significant. Personal pensions in their current form were introduced in 1988.

- Investment income was received by 62 per cent of all pensioners in 2016/17. The percentage of pensioners in receipt has decreased over the past 20 years, from 71 per cent in 1996/97. This difference is statistically significant. The decrease between 2006/07 and 2016/17 was predominantly in 2010/11 to 2012/13. This period follows the financial crisis, which started in 2008.

- Overall 17 per cent of pensioners were in receipt of earnings in 2016/17, compared to 11 percent in 1996/97. This is a statistically significant increase. This includes pensioner couples where one partner was under SPa.

See overleaf for a summary of important facts.

SUMMARY OF IMPORTANT FACTS

State Pension

Almost all pensioners (97 per cent) received income from State Pension, with an average income of £167. Twenty per cent of those in receipt had an income of over £250.

Income-related benefits

Twenty-four per cent of pensioners were in receipt of income-related benefits. Of those in receipt the average income was £77.

Disability benefits

Twenty-one per cent of pensioners were in receipt of disability benefits and the average income was £81. Some benefits have set rates, which may explain peaks in the distribution. For example, Attendance Allowance has a lower rate of £55.10 and a higher rate of £82.30.

Private pension

Seventy-one per cent of pensioners received income from a private pension with an average amount of £158. Fourteen per cent of those in receipt had an income of over £500.

Occupational pension

Over half of all pensioners (62 per cent) were in receipt of an occupational pension and the average amount was £161. Fourteen per cent of those in receipt had an occupational pension income of over £500.

Personal pension

Nineteen per cent of pensioners had income from a personal pension with an average of £51. Twenty-three per cent of pensioners in receipt had a personal pension income of less than £20.

Investments

Sixty-two per cent of pensioners were in receipt of investment income with an average income of £6. Six per cent of pensioners had a weekly income of over £250.

Earnings

Seventeen per cent of pensioners were in receipt of earnings with an average income of £322. Fifteen per cent of pensioners had an income of over £1,000 per week.

Amongst other things, the above illustrates that those in the poorest and wealthiest bands have a wide gap in income, in particular in the areas of earnings and investments. The richest have managed to ensure that there is enough money in the pot to cater for retirement. Those in the lower income bands rely heavily on state pensions and other benefits. The Pensioners Income Series measures those within the bottom, middle and top fifth of the population.

For more information on the Pensioner Income Series you should go to www.gov.uk/government/collection/pensioners-income-series-statistics-july-2016/17. There is a whole array of comparisons and general information, most of it quite interesting.

*****

Chapter 2

How Much Income is needed in Retirement-Planning Ahead

When attempting to forecast for future pension needs, there are a number of factors which need to be taken into account:

These are:

- Your income needs in retirement and how much of that income you can expect to derive from state pensions
- How much pension that any savings you have will produce
- How long you have to save for
- Projected inflation

Income needs in retirement

This is very much a personal decision and will be influenced by a number of factors, such as ongoing housing costs, care costs, projected lifestyle etc. The main factor is that you have enough to live on comfortably. In retirement you will probably take more holidays and want to enjoy your free time. This costs money so your future planning should take into account all your projected needs and costs. When calculating future needs, all sources of income should be taken into account.

What period to save over

The obvious fact is that, the longer period that you save over the more you will build up and hence the more that you will have in retirement. As time goes on savings are compounded and the value of the pot goes up. One thing is for certain and that is if you leave it too late then you will have to put away a large slice of your income to produce a decent pension. If you plan to retire at an early age then you will need to save more to produce the same benefits.

Inflation

As prices rise, so your money buys you less. This is the main effect of inflation and to maintain the same level of spending power you will need to save more as time goes on. Many forms of retirement plans will include a calculation for inflation. Currently, inflation is at 2.7% (January 2019) expected to fall to 2.1% by the third quarter. However, history shows that the effects of inflation can be corrosive, having risen above 25% per annum in the past. Hopefully, this is now under control

For most people, retirement is a substantial part of life, probably lasting a couple of decades or more. It follows that ensuring your financial security in retirement requires some forward planning. Developing a plan calls for a general review of your current finances and careful consideration of how you can build up your savings to generate the retirement income that you need.

There are five distinct stages to planning your retirement which are summarised below.

Stage 1-this involves checking first that other aspects of your basic finances are in good shape. Planning for retirement generally means locking away your money for a long time. Once invested it is usually impossible to get pension savings back early, even in an emergency. It is therefore essential that you have other more accessible savings available for emergencies and that you do not have any problem debts that could tip you into a financial crisis. You must then weigh up saving for retirement against other goals that are more pressing, such as making sure that your household would be financially secure if you were unable to work because of illness or the main breadwinner dies.

Stage 2-You need to decide how much income you might need when you retire. There is a table overleaf which might help you in calculating this.

Stage 3- Check how much pension that you have built up so far.

Stage 4-Compare your amount from stage 3 with your target income from stage 2.

Stage 5-Review your progress once a year and/or if your circumstances change.

It is a fact that many people need far less in retirement than when actively working. The expenses that exist when working, such as mortgage payments, children and work related expenses do not exist when retired. The average household between 30-49 spends £473 per week and £416 between 50-

64. This drops to £263 per week between 65 to 74 and even lower in later retirement (Expenditure and Food Survey).

However, as might be expected, expenditure on health care increases correspondingly with age. Whilst the state may help with some costs the individual still has to bear a high proportion of expenditure on health related items. When calculating how much money you will need in retirement, it is useful to use a table in order to list your anticipated expenses as follows

Everyday needs

Item	Annual Total
Food and other	
Leisure (newspapers etc)	
Pets	
Clothes	
Other household items	
Gardening	
General expenses	
Home expenses	
Mortgage/rent	
Service charges/repairs	
Insurance	
Council tax	
Water and other utilities	
Telephone	
TV licence other charges (satellite)	
Other expenses (home help)	

Leisure and general entertainment

Hobbies	

Eating out	
Cinema/theatre	
Holidays	
Other luxuries (smoking/drinking	

Transport

Car expenses	
Car hire	
Petrol etc	
Bus/train fares	

Health

Dental charges	
Optical expenses	
Medical insurance	
Care insurance	
Other health related expenses	

Anniversaries/birthdays etc

Children/grandchildren	
Relatives other than children	
Christmas	
Charitable donations	
Other expenses	

Savings and loans

General savings	
Saving for later retirement	
Other savings	
Loan repayments	

Other

The above should give you an idea of the amounts that you will need per annum to live well. Obviously, you should plan for a monthly income that will meet those needs. You should also take account of income tax on your retirement incomes.

The impact of inflation

When you are planning for many years ahead, it is essential to take account of the effects of inflation. Currently, at the time of writing in 2019, we are in a period of relatively low inflation, 1.8% in the first quarter expected to decrease by the third quarter, largely due to low oil prices (however, watch out for the BREXIT effect, whatever that may be). As prices rise over the years, the money we will have will buy less and less. For example, in the extreme case, if prices double then a fixed amount of money will buy only half as much. The higher the rate of inflation, the more you have to save to reach your income target. The table below will give you an idea of the changes in rates of inflation over the last ten years to 2019.

ear	jan	feb	mar	apr	may	jun	jul	aug	sep	oct	nov	dec	ann
2019	1.8%												
2018	3%	2.7%	2.4%	2.4%	2.4%	2.4%	2.5%	2.6%	2.4%	2.4%	2.3%	2.1%	2.5%
2017	1.8%	2.3%	2.3%	2.7%	2.9%	2.7%	2.6%	2.9%	2.9%	3%	3.1%	2.9%	2.7%
2016	0.3%	0.3%	0.5%	0.3%	0.3%	0.4%	0.6%	0.6%	1%	0.9%	1.2%	1.6%	0.7%
2015	0.3%	0%	0%	-0.2%	0.1%	0%	0.1%	0.1%	-0.1%	-0.1%	0.2%	0.2%	0%
2014	2%	1.7%	1.6%	1.8%	1.5%	1.9%	1.6%	1.5%	1.2%	1.3%	0.9%	0.5%	1.5%
2013	2.6%	2.8%	2.8%	2.4%	2.7%	2.9%	2.8%	2.7%	2.7%	2.2%	2.1%	2%	2.6%
2012	3.6%	3.4%	3.5%	3%	2.7%	2.4%	2.5%	2.5%	2.2%	2.6%	2.7%	2.6%	2.8%
2011	4%	4.3%	3.9%	4.5%	4.5%	4.2%	4.5%	4.5%	5.1%	5%	4.8%	4.3%	4.5%
2010	3.4%	3%	3.4%	3.7%	3.5%	3.2%	3%	3.2%	3.1%	3.2%	3.2%	3.6%	3.3%
2009	3%	3.1%	2.9%	2.4%	2.1%	1.8%	1.9%	1.5%	1.2%	1.5%	2%	2.9%	2

Some pension schemes give you automatic protection against inflation, but many don't and it is largely up to you to decide what protection to build into your planning. The first step is to be aware what effect inflation might have. Fortunately, pension statements and projections these days must all be adjusted for inflation so that figures you are given are expressed in today's money. This gives you an idea of the standard of living you might expect and helps you assess the amount that you need to save. Providers of non-pension investments (such as unit trusts and investment trusts (see later chapters) do not have to give you statements and projections adjusted for inflation. If you use these other investments for your retirement then you will have to make your own adjustments. You can do this using the table below.

Value in today's money of £1,000 you receive in the future

Average rate of inflation

Number of years until you receive the money	2.5% a year	5% a year	7.5% a year	10% a year
5	£884	£784	£697	£621
10	£781	£614	£485	£386
15	£690	£481	£338	£239
20	£610	£377	£235	£149
25	£539	£295	£164	£92
30	£477	£231	£114	£57
35	£421	£181	£80	£36
40	£372	£142	£55	£22
45	£329	£111	£39	£14
50	£291	£87	£39	£9

The above should be a good guide. If you require more detailed forecasting you should go to www.ons.gov.uk (Office of National Statistics).

In the next chapters we will be discussing the various sources of pensions, starting with the all-important State Pension.

****

Chapter 3

Sources of Pensions-A Summary

Sources of pension savings- The State Pension

We will be elaborating on the State Pension further in chapter 4. In brief, the State Pension system is based on National Insurance contributions, payments made by an individual which funds today's pension payments and for those who are young the future contributions will foot their pension bill. Therefore, the state pension system is not a savings scheme it is a pay-as-you-go system.

Pensions are a major area of government spending and are becoming more and more so. Protecting pensions against inflationary increases have put pressure on respective governments, along with the introduction of a second tier-pension, the State second pension (S2P).

The problems of pension provision are set to increase with the numbers of older people outnumbering those in active work, leading to an imbalance in provision. The biggest dilemma facing the government, and future governments, is the problem of convincing people to save for their pensions, therefore taking some of the burden off the state.

As we have seen from the statistics in the previous chapter, those most at risk in terms of retirement poverty are the lower earners, who quite often do not build up enough contributions to gain a state pension, those who contribute to a state pension but cannot save enough to contribute to a private scheme and disabled people who cannot work or carers who also cannot work. The above is not an exclusive list. The government has recognised the difficulties faced by these groups and has, along the way, introduced the state second pension and pension credits.

The over 80 pension

This is a non-contributory pension for people aged 80 or over with little or no state pension. If you are 80 or over, not getting or getting a reduced state pension because you have not paid enough National Insurance contributions (NI) and are currently living in England, Scotland or Wales and have been doing so for a total of 10 years or more in any continuous period of 20 years before or after your 80th birthday, you could claim the over 80 pension. The maximum amount of the over 80 state pension that you can get is currently £75.50 per week (2018/19).

Occupational pensions

We discuss occupational pension schemes in more depth later in this book. Briefly, occupational pension schemes are a very important source of income. With Occupational pension schemes the contract is between the company and the pension provider. With Group Personal Pension Schemes, which we will also be discussing later, although the employer chooses the company the contract is between the employee and the pension company.

Occupational pension Schemes are one of the best ways to pay into a pension scheme as the employer has to contribute a significant amount to the pot. Over the years the amounts paid into occupational pension schemes has increased significantly. Although there have been a number of incidences of occupational schemes being wound up this is relatively small and they remain a key source of retirement income.

From October 2012, it has been compulsory for employers to provide an occupational pension scheme, Auto Enrolment. For the first time, employers are obliged to:

- enrol most of their workforce into a pension scheme; and
- make employer pension contributions

This affects all employers in the UK, regardless of the number of individuals that they employ. Anyone who is classed as a 'worker' for National Minimum Wage purposes is included in the new pension regime.

This has been introduced in stages, and each employer was given a 'staging date' determined by how many employees they had as at April 1st 2012. We will be discussing Auto Enrolment further in chapter 7.

Stakeholder schemes

Stakeholder pension schemes are designed for those people who do not have an employer, or had an employer who did not have an occupational scheme. They therefore cannot pay into an occupational scheme. If an employer did not offer an occupational scheme (many small employers were exempt) they had to arrange access to a stakeholder scheme. Employees did not have to join an occupational scheme offered by employers, instead they could join a stakeholder scheme. Likewise, self-employed people can also join a stakeholder scheme.

Stakeholder schemes have a contribution limit-this being currently £3,600 per year. Anyone who is not earning can also pay into a scheme, up to the limit above. You pay money to a pension provider (eg an insurance company, bank or building society) who invests it (eg in shares).These are a type of personal pension but they have to meet some minimum standards set by the government. These include:

- management charges can't be more than 1.5% of the fund's value for the first 10 years and 1% after that
- you must be able to start and stop payments when you want or switch providers without being charged
- they have to meet certain security standards, eg have independent trustees and auditors.

How much can be invested in a stakeholder pension?
There is no limit to the amount that can be invested in a stakeholder pension scheme. However, tax relief can only be obtained on contributions up to a maximum annual contribution limit (known as an individual's 'annual allowance'). For the tax year 2019/20, this is set at the lower of 100% of an individual's UK earnings or £40,000 per annum. Carry forward of unused allowances may be permitted in some circumstances. It is possible to contribute up to £3,600 per year (including tax relief) into a stakeholder pension scheme even if a person is not earning. A member of an occupational pension scheme may also contribute to a stakeholder pension scheme. You can start making payments into a stakeholder pension from £20 per month. You can pay

weekly or monthly. If you don't want to make regular payments you can pay lump sums any time you want.

The rules for stakeholder pensions changed on 1 October 2012. If you're starting a new job now or returning to one, your employer doesn't have to offer you access to a stakeholder pension scheme. They now have to offer entry through automatic enrolment. If you're in a stakeholder pension scheme that was arranged by your employer before 1 October 2012, they must continue to take and pay contributions from your wages. This arrangement is in place until:

- you ask them to stop
- you stop paying contributions at regular intervals
- you leave your job

If you leave your job or change to another personal pension, the money they have paid in stays in your pension pot unless you have it transferred to a different pension provider.

Other ways to save for retirement

The government offers certain tax advantages to encourage pension saving. However, the most advantageous savings plan is the Individual Savings Account (ISA) discussed further on in the book. In addition, you might have regular savings accounts, your home or a second home. All of these possibilities must be factored in when arriving at an adequate retirement income.

Chapter 4

The State Pension

Over 97% of pensioners receive the basic state pension. (Pensioners Income Series 2016/2017). Therefore, it is here to stay. Everyone who has paid the appropriate national insurance contributions will be entitled to a state pension. If you are not working you can either receive pension credits, as discussed, or make voluntary contributions.

The full state pension is £125.95 for a single person and £251.90 (2018/2019) for a couple. From April 2016, for men who were born after 6th April 1951 and women who were born after 6th April 1953 the pension is £164.35 per week (2018/2019). This is known as a 'flat rate' or 'single tier' system and is designed to make the current system more simple and easier to understand. Getting the flat rate however, is very much dependant on contributions.

Basic state pensions are increased each April in line with price inflation. State pensioners also receive a (£10 Christmas bonus-check current entitlement) and are entitled to winter fuel payments. Married women can claim a pension based on their spouse's NI record. Men who have reached 65 are also able to claim a basic state pension based on their wife's contribution record where the wife reaches state pension age on or after 6th April 2010.

Same sex couples, as a result of the Civil Partnerships Act 2004, along with married couples of the same sex, following the passing of the Marriage (Same sex Couples Act) 2014, have the same rights as heterosexual couples in all aspects of pension provision.

Transsexual people

Your State Pension might be affected if you're a transsexual person.

Transgender people born between 24 December 1919 and 3 April 1945 may be affected by court judgements about State Pension entitlement and liability to pay National Insurance contributions.

The Gender Recognition Act 2004 gave transgender people the opportunity to legally change gender by applying for a Gender Recognition Certificate.

The Gender Recognition Act 2004 came into force on 4 April 2005. Transgender people who reached 60 before this date, and who meet certain conditions, can claim equal treatment rights for social security purposes and could get backdated State Pension. The period for equal treatment starts from age 60 or the date of gender reassignment surgery, whichever is the latest. A Court of Appeal decision established the qualifying conditions.

Transgender people who do not satisfy the equal treatment eligibility criteria or do not have a Gender Recognition Certificate can only claim State Pension in their birth gender.

Claiming equal treatment rights for State Pension

You can claim equal treatment rights for periods before the Gender Recognition Act 2004 came into force if you:

- were born 24 December 1919 to 3 April 1945
- can provide evidence of relevant gender reassignment surgery that took place before 4 April 2005

If you meet both of these conditions, you can ask for an 'expression of interest' form from The Pension Service.

How many qualifying years do you need to get the full State Pension?

The number of qualifying years you need to get a full state pension depends on when you reach your State Pension age. If you reached State Pension age before 6 April 2010, you normally needed 44 qualifying years if you are a man, or 39 qualifying years if you are woman. If you reach State Pension age on or after 6 April 2010 but before 6 April 2016, you need 30 qualifying years. If you reach State Pension age on or after 6 April 2016, you normally need 35 qualifying years.

Using someone else's contribution record

In some circumstances, you may be able to use your husband's, wife's or civil partner's contribution record to help you qualify for a State Pension.

(see overleaf about National Insurance Contributions)

NI contributions counting towards a basic state pension.

Type of contribution	Paid by	Details for 2016-17
No Contributions but earnings between LEL and PT	Employees	If you earn between the Lower Earning Limit and the Primary Threshold you will get National Insurance 'credits' – that is you will be entitled to some basic National Insurance benefits, but won't actually pay any National Insurance. These limits are respectively £116 and £162 per week for 2018/19 .
Class 1 full rate on earnings between PT and UAP	Employees	Earnings between £162 and £892. usually paid at 12% but less if contracted out (see further on)
Class 2	Self-employed	Flat rate of £2.95 per week. Those with earnings for the year of less than £6205 can choose to opt out
Class 3	Out of the labour market and not receiving NI credits	Flat rate of £14.65per week

Key to abbreviations

LEL = Lower earnings limit: PT = Primary Threshold: UAP = Upper Accruals Point: UEL = Upper earnings limit. LEL, PT and UEL usually increase each year UAP is fixed.

Class 1 contributions-Class 1 contributions are paid if earnings are above the primary threshold. The Threshold, set by government annually, is currently £162 per week (tax year 2018/19). If your earnings are above this set limit then you will be paying contributions at class 1 that build up to a state pension. The level of contribution is set at 12% of earnings above the primary threshold level up to an upper earnings limit which is £892 per week in 2018/19. Contributions are paid at 2% of earnings above the upper earnings limit. If a person earns less than the primary threshold they will not pay NI contributions. The year will still count towards building up a basic state pension provided the earnings are not less than the lower earnings limit. This is £116 at 2018/19.

Class 2 contributions-Self-employed people will build up their NI contributions by paying class 2 contributions. These are paid either by direct debit or by quarterly bill at the rate of £2.95 per week (2018/19). If you are a director of your own company then class 1 contributions will be paid and not class 2.

Class 3 contributions-If a person is not paying class 1 or 2 contributions or receiving HRP they can pay class 3 voluntary contributions. These are charged at a flat rate of £14.65 per week (2018/19). They can be paid up to 6 years back to make up any shortfall.

Class 4 Contributions-Class 4 NICs are for self-employed people whose net profits are over a certain amount. Class 4 National Insurance contributions are paid in addition to the flat rate of Class 2 National Insurance contributions. These contributions are profit-related, so unlike Class 2, not all self-employed people will have to pay them. *Class 4 contributions do not count towards benefit entitlement.*

Pension credits

Pension credits began life in October 2003. The credit is designed to top up the resources of pensioners whose income is low. The pension credit has two components: a guarantee credit and a saving credit.

The Guarantee credit

This is available to anyone over a qualifying age (equal to women's state pension age-see further on) whose income is less than a set amount called the minimum guarantee. The guarantee will bring income up to £163 for a single person and £248.80 for a couple (including same sex couples) (2018-2019). The minimum guarantee is higher for certain categories of disabled people and carers. The qualifying age for Pension Credit is gradually going up to 66 in line with the increase in the State Pension age for women to 65 and the further increase to 66 for men and women.

The Savings credit

Savings Credit is extra money if you've got some savings or your income is higher than the basic State Pension. It's only available to people who reached State Pension age before 6 April 2016. You could get up to:

- £13.40 extra per week if you're single
- or £14.99 if you're a couple.

Am I entitled to Savings Credit?

Only people who've reached State Pension age before 6 April 2016 may be eligible to claim the Savings Credit part of Pension Credit.

- If you're a couple and one of you reached State Pension age before 6 April 2016, you may be able to claim.

- There isn't a savings limit for Pension Credit, but if you have over £10,000 this will affect how much you receive.

The income taken into account for savings credit is the same as for guarantee credit, but various types of income are now ignored. These are Working Tax Credit, contribution-based Employment and Support Allowance, Incapacity Benefit, contribution-based Jobseeker's Allowance, Severe Disablement Allowance, Maternity Allowance and maintenance payments made to you (child maintenance is always ignored).

If your income is still over the savings threshold, the Pension Service works out your entitlement to savings credit.

If you don't qualify for guarantee credit, you can still get savings credit at a reduced rate to reflect the fact that your income exceeds the minimum level the law says you need to live on. The same steps as above are taken to work out your entitlement, but the Pension Service will also calculate how much your income is above the appropriate minimum guarantee used for guarantee credit. Your savings credit award will be reduced by 40% of the difference.

If you reach State Pension age on or after 6 April 2016

Most people who reach State Pension age on or after 6 April 2016 won't be eligible for Savings Credit.

But you may continue to get Savings Credit if both of the following apply:

- you're in a couple and one of you reached State Pension age before 6 April 2016
- you were getting Savings Credit up to 6 April 2016

If you stop being eligible for Savings Credit for any reason from 6 April 2016, you won't be able to get it again.

National Insurance Credits

In some situations you may get National Insurance Credits, which plug what would otherwise be gaps in your NI record. You might get credits in the following situations.

- when you are unemployed, or unable to work because you are ill, and claiming certain benefits
- If you were aged 16 to 18 before 6 April 2010, you were usually credited automatically with National Insurance credits. No new awards will be made from 6 April 2010.
- if you are on an approved training course
- when you are doing jury service
- if you are getting Statutory Adoption Pay, Statutory Maternity Pay, Additional Statutory Paternity Pay, Statutory Sick Pay, Maternity Allowance or Working Tax Credit
- if you have been wrongly put in prison

- if you are caring for a child or for someone who is sick or disabled
- if you are aged 16 or over and provided care for a child under 12, that you are related to and you lived in the UK for the period(s) of care
- if your spouse or civil partner is a member of Her Majesty's forces and you are accompanying them on an assignment outside the UK

There are special arrangements for people who worked or were detained without pay in Iraq during the Gulf Crisis. If you think you might be affected by this, write to HM Revenue & Customs (HMRC) at:

HM Revenue & Customs
National Insurance Contributions & Employer Office
Benton Park View
Newcastle upon Tyne
NE98 1ZZ
0300 200 3310

The State Pension age

Currently, the state pension age is 65 for men. On 6th April 2010, the state pension age for women started to increase gradually from 60-65, to match men's. There will be further increases in the state pension age to 68 for men and women. The increase in the State Pension age is being phased in and your own particular pension age depends on when you were born. The proposed changes affect people born between April 1953 and 5th April 1960. (For your own retirement age you should go to the Pensions Service Website).

Additional state pension

S2P replaced the State Earnings Related Pension (SERPS) in April 2002. SERPS was, essentially, a state second tier pension and it was compulsory to pay into this in order to supplement the basic state pension. There were drawbacks however, and many people fell through the net so S2P was introduced to allow other groups to contribute. S2P refined SERPS allowing the following to contribute:

- People caring for children under six and entitled to child benefit

- Carers looking after someone who is elderly or disabled, if they are entitled to carers allowance

- Certain people who are unable to work because of illness or disability, if they are entitled to long-term incapacity benefit or severe disablement allowance and they have been in the workforce for at least one-tenth of their working life

Self-employed people are excluded from S2P as are employees earning less than the lower earnings limit. Married women and widows paying class 1 contributions at the reduced rate do not build up additional state pension. S2P is an earnings related scheme. This means that people on high earnings build up more pension than those on lower earnings. However, people earning at least the lower earnings limit (£116) in 2018/19 but less than the low earnings threshold (£162) in 2018/19 are treated as if they have earnings at that level and so build up more pension than they otherwise would.

Contracting out

A person does not build up state additional pension during periods when they are contracted out. Contracting out means that a person has opted to join an occupational scheme or a personal pensions scheme or stakeholder pension. While contacted out, a person will pay lower National Insurance Contributions on part of earnings or some of the contributions paid by an employee and employer are 'rebated' and paid into the occupational pension scheme or other pension scheme.

Increasing your state pension

There are a number of ways in which you can increase your State Pension, particularly if you have been presented with a pension forecast which shows lack of contributions and a diminished state pension. You can fill gaps in your pension contributions or you can defer your state pension. HM Revenue and Customs have a help line on 0300 200 3300 to check your record and to receive advice on whether you have gaps and how to fill them.

Gaps in pension contributions

The changes in State Pension means that in order to qualify for the new single-tier pension, you need a minimum of 10 qualifying years of contributions, either by paying National Insurance Contributions or Credits. In order to be entitled for the maximum amount, you will need at least 35 qualifying years, again through contributions or credits.

People who have gaps in their National Insurance (NI) record, because they lived abroad or were employed/self-employed with low earnings or profits, can make up for the shortfall by making voluntary NI contributions. However, it is important to understand which type of voluntary contribution is available to you.

There are two types of voluntary NI contribution.

Class 3A Lump Sum Payment

If you are entitled to a UK State pension and you reached State pension age before 5th April 2016 (i.e. men born before 6th April 1951 and women born before 6 April 1953), you can top up the amount of Additional State pension you receive by making a Class 3A lump sum payment. This must be made before 5th April 2023, and the amount can be increased from £1 to £25 per week.

The amount of the lump sum payment will depend on how much extra per week is required as well as how old you are; the older the person is, the less it costs. Once the payment is received, then the higher pension amount is paid from that date. Note there is a 90-day cooling off period if you change your mind.

Class 3 Contributions

If you don't have the full number of qualifying years to receive the full State pension, then you can make a Class 3 contribution. The current rate of Class 3 contributions is £14.10 a week

Class 3 contributions can usually be made to fill gaps in the last 6 years before your state pension entitlement. There is an exception to this, as up until the end of this tax year you can fill gaps in the last seven years.

Class 2 Contributions

If you are under State pension age, self-employed, with earnings below the small profits threshold (£6205 for 2018/19 tax year) and you wish to make voluntary contributions, you would usually pay Class 2 contributions. These pay for your State pension and some other State benefits, and the rate is much less at £2.95 per week (in the current tax year 2018/2019).

In summary, Class 3A contributions are for those people wanting to top up their Additional State pension which they are already in receipt of, and Class 3 contributions are for those who want to increase the number of qualifying years they have on record.

Deferring your state pension-How it works

You don't get your State Pension automatically - you have to claim it. You should get a letter no later than 2 months before you reach State Pension age, telling you what to do.

You can either claim your State Pension or delay (defer) claiming it.

If you want to defer, you don't have to do anything. Your pension will automatically be deferred until you claim it.

Deferring your State Pension could increase the payments you get when you decide to claim it. Any extra payments you get from deferring could be taxed.

If you're on benefits

You can't get extra State Pension if you get certain benefits. Deferring can also affect how much you can get in benefits.
You must tell the Pension Service if you're on benefits and you want to defer.

What you'll get

The amount of extra State Pension you could get depends on when you reach State Pension age.

If you reach State Pension age on or after 6 April 2016

Your State Pension will increase every week you defer, as long as you defer for at least 9 weeks.

Your State Pension increases by the equivalent of 1% for every 9 weeks you defer. This works out as just under 5.8% for every full year.

The extra amount is paid with your regular State Pension payment.

Example: You get £164.35 a week (the full new State Pension). This works out as £8,546.20 a year.

By deferring for one year, you'll get an extra £493 a year (just under 5.8% of £8,546.20).

This example assumes there is no annual increase in the State Pension. If there is an annual increase, the amount you could get could be larger.

If you reached State Pension age before 6 April 2016

You can usually take your extra State Pension as either:

- higher weekly payments
- a one-off lump sum

When you claim your deferred State Pension, you'll get a letter asking how you want to take your extra pension. You'll have 3 months from receiving that letter to decide.

Higher weekly payments

Your State Pension will increase every week you defer, as long as you defer for at least 5 weeks.

Your State Pension increases by the equivalent of 1% for every 5 weeks you defer. This works out as 10.4% for every full year.

The extra amount is paid with your regular State Pension payment.

Example: You get £125.95 a week (the full basic State Pension). This works out as £6,549.40 a year.

By deferring for one year, you'll get an extra £681 a year (10.4% of £6,549.40).

This example assumes there is no annual increase in the State Pension. If there is an annual increase, the amount you could get could be larger.

Lump sum payment

You can get a one-off lump sum payment if you defer claiming your State Pension for at least 12 months in a row. This will include interest of 2% above the Bank of England base rate.

If you're in prison

You won't build up extra State Pension until you leave prison.

Annual increases

After you claim your State Pension, the extra amount you get because you deferred will usually increase each year based on the Consumer Price Index. It won't increase for some people who live abroad.

If you get benefits or tax credits

You can't build up extra State Pension during any period you get:

- Income Support
- Pension Credit

- Employment and Support Allowance (income-related)
- Jobseeker's Allowance (income-based)
- Universal Credit
- Carer's Allowance
- Incapacity Benefit
- Severe Disablement Allowance
- Widow's Pension
- Widowed Parent's Allowance
- Unemployability Supplement

You can't build up extra State Pension during any period your partner gets:
- Income Support
- Pension Credit
- Universal Credit
- Employment and Support Allowance (income-related)
- Jobseeker's Allowance (income-related)

Higher weekly payments

Taking your extra State Pension as higher weekly payments could reduce the amount you get from:
- Income Support
- Pension Credit
- Universal Credit
- Employment and Support Allowance (income-related)
- Jobseeker's Allowance (income-related)
- Housing Benefit
- Council Tax Reduction
- tax credits

If you reached State Pension age before 6 April 2016

Your tax credits or Universal Credit payments may be reduced if you choose to take your extra State Pension as a lump sum.

Winter Fuel Payment

You need to claim Winter Fuel Payment if you've deferred your State Pension. You only need to do this once.

Claim a deferred State Pension

There are 4 ways to claim:

- online
- download the State Pension claim form and send it to your local pension centre
- claim from abroad (including the Channel Islands)
- over the phone

State Pension claim line

Telephone: 0800 731 7898

Textphone: 0800 731 7339

Monday to Friday, 8am to 6pm (except public holidays)

Inheriting a deferred State Pension

You can usually inherit your partner's extra State Pension if all of the following apply:

- your partner reached State Pension age before 6 April 2016
- you were married to, or in a civil partnership with, your partner when they died
- your partner had deferred their State Pension or was claiming their deferred State Pension when they died

- you didn't remarry or form a new civil partnership before you reached State Pension age
- If your partner died before 6 April 2010, one of the following must also apply:
- you were over State Pension age when your partner died
- you were under State Pension age when your partner died, you're a woman and your deceased partner was your husband

You can only receive any extra State Pension you've inherited once you've reached State Pension age.

If your partner died before claiming their State Pension

How you inherit your partner's extra State Pension depends on how long they deferred their pension for.

A year or more

If your partner deferred their State Pension by a year or more, you can usually choose to inherit it as a lump sum or as weekly payments. You'll get a letter with the options you can choose from.

Between 5 weeks and a year

If your partner deferred their State Pension by between 5 weeks and a year, you'll inherit it as weekly payments. You'll get these payments with your own State Pension.

Less than 5 weeks

If your partner deferred their State Pension by less than 5 weeks, their State Pension payments for those weeks will become part their estate (their total property, money and possessions).

If your partner was getting their extra State Pension before they died

You'll inherit your partner's extra State Pension as extra weekly payments. You'll get these payments with your own State Pension.

Women and Pensions

It is a general rule that women pensioners tend to have less income than their male counterparts. Therefore, when building a retirement plan, women need to consider what steps they and their partners can take to make their financial future more secure.

Particular issues for women

These days, the rules of any particular pension scheme-whether state or private, do not discriminate between men and women. Whether male or female you pay the same to access the same level of benefits. However, this does not always mean that women end up with the same level of pension as men. This is because of the general working and lifestyle differences between men and women, for example women are more likely to take breaks from work and take part time work so they can look after family. As a result, women are more likely to pay less into a pension fund than men.

Historically, the (idealised) role of women as carers was built into the UK pensions system. Not least the state pension system. It was assumed that women would marry before having children and rely on their husbands to provide for them financially right through to retirement. As a result, women who have already retired typically have much lower incomes than men. Changes to the state scheme for people reaching state pension age from 6th April 2010 onwards, mean that most women will, in future, retire with similar state pensions as men. However if you are an unmarried women living with a partner you should be aware of the following:

The state scheme recognises wives, husbands and civil partners but not unmarried partners. This means that if your unmarried partner dies before you, you would not be eligible for the state benefits that provide support for bereaved dependants.

- Occupational schemes and personal pensions typically pay survivor benefits to a bereaved partner, whether married or not. However many schemes-especially in the public sector-have recognised unmarried partners only recently and, as a result, the survivor pension for an unmarried partner may be very low.
- The legal system recognises that wives, husbands and civil partners may have a claim on retirement savings built up by the other party in the event of divorce, but these will be considered along with all the other assets to be split between you and you may end up with a much lower retirement income than you had been expecting.
- The legal system does not give similar rights to unmarried partners who split up. If your unmarried partner was building up pension savings for you both, he or she can walk away with all those savings and you have no legal claim on them.

Effects of changes to the state pension from 2016 on women

As we have discussed, from April 2016, the new "flat rate " state pension will typically be £164.35 a week (2018/19), but only for those who have paid national insurance contributions (NIC's) for 35 years. Many women will not qualify, having taken career breaks to care for children.

If there are gaps in your entitlement then consider buying some added years of state pension which you can do in the run-up to retirement. The state pension purchase scheme is far more generous than any private pension, provided you live more than a few years in retirement. Be careful, though, that you're not going to be buying years that you'd actually make up through work between now and retirement, otherwise you could end up giving the government money for something you'd have got anyway. Voluntary NIC's cost £14.65 (class 3) a week or £761.80 a year, and you can normally fill gaps from the past six years. If you are due to retire after April 2016, check to see how much you will receive at gov.uk/future-pension-centre.

Have you told the government you are a carer?

The good news is that full-time unpaid carers will be entitled to the same pension as those who have worked in a paid full-time job from 2016. However, thousands of women who do not claim child benefit or carers' allowance could miss out.

These benefits signal to the Department for Work and Pensions (DWP) that an individual qualifies for NIC's. Since households earning above £50,000 are no longer eligible to claim full child benefit, and those earning over £60,000 will receive no child benefit at all, many stay-at home mums may go under the radar. Similarly if women are caring for a family member but not claiming carer's allowance their unpaid work will go unrecognised. If you are a carer but don't claim any benefits pro-actively contact the DWP to report your situation. If your household income is over £50,000 but under £60,000 you should still register for child benefit in order to receive NIC's.

****

Chapter 5

Private Pension Savings-General

The lifetime allowance

There is a single lifetime limit on the amount of savings that a person can build up through various pension schemes and plans that are subject to tax relief. (This excludes the state pension). The lifetime allowance is £1,030,000m from April 2018.

The lifetime allowance applies to savings in all types of pension schemes including occupational pensions and stakeholder schemes. There are, broadly, two types of scheme or plan:

- Defined contribution-with these types of schemes money goes in and is invested with the fund used to buy a pension. Basically, if the fund at retirement is £200,000 then £200,000 lifetime allowance has been used up

- Defined benefit-in this type of scheme, a person is promised a pension of a certain amount usually worked out on the basis of salary before retirement and the length of time that you have been in the scheme. The equation for working out lifetime benefit in this type of scheme is a little more complicated. The pension is first converted into a notional sum (the amount of money it is reckoned is needed to buy a pension of that size). The government sets out a factor that it says will be needed to make the conversion which it has said is 20. If the pension is £20,000 then this is calculated as £20,000 times £20,000 which is £400,000. Therefore £400,000 will be used up from the lifetime allowance.

Protecting the Lifetime Allowance

The standard lifetime allowance was reduced to:

- £1,030,000 million on 6 April 2018

But you may be able to protect your pension(s) from these reductions. There are 3 protections you can apply for.

See table overleaf

Protection	What it does	Can I keep building up my pension(s)?
Individual protection 2016	Protects your lifetime allowance to the lower of: - the value of your pension(s) at 5 April 2016- £1.25 million	Yes. But you must pay tax on money taken from your pension(s) that exceed your protected lifetime allowance.
Fixed protection 2016	Fixes your lifetime allowance at £1.25 million.	No, except in limited circumstances. If you do, you'll: - lose your fixed protection 2016 - pay tax on any pension(s) above the standard lifetime allowance when you take your pension
Individual protection 2014	Protects your lifetime allowance to the lower of: - the value of your pension(s) at 5 April 2014 - £1.5 million	Yes. But you must pay tax on money taken from your pension(s) that exceed your protected lifetime allowance.

For more detailed information about Pension protection Schemes go to: www.gov.uk/guidance/pension-schemes-protect-your-lifetime-allowance

The annual allowance

The annual allowance (amount that an individual can contribute to a pension) is £40,000 (April 2019). This is the amount that pension savings may increase each year whether through contributions paid in or to promised benefits. In addition, you can carry forward unused allowances from three years previously   The annual allowance will not start in the year a person starts their pension or die. This gives a person scope to make large last-minute additions to their fund. If at retirement the value of a pension exceeds the lifetime allowance there will be an income tax charge of 55% on the excess if it is taken as a lump sum, or 25% if it is left in the scheme to be taken as a pension, which is taxable as income. If the increase in the value of savings in any year exceeds the annual allowance, the excess is taxed at 40%.

Limits to benefits and contributions

The present benefit and contribution limits have been scrapped. The only remaining restrictions are:

- Contributions-the maximum that can be paid in each year is either the amount equal to taxable earnings or £3,600 whichever is the greater

- Tax free lump sum-at retirement a person can take up to one quarter of the value of the total pension fund as a tax free lump sum

Taking a pension

Savings do not have to be converted into pension in one go. This can be staggered and pension income can be increased as a person winds down from work.

For each tranche of pension started before 75, there is a range of choices. This will depend on the rules of each individual scheme. A person can:

- Have a pension paid direct from an occupational pension scheme
- Use a pension fund to purchase an annuity to provide a pension for the rest of life
- Use part of the pension to buy a limited period annuity lasting just five years leaving the rest invested
- Opt for income drawdown which allows taking of a pension whilst leaving the rest invested. The tax-free lump sum could be taken and the rest left invested. The maximum income will be 120% of a standard annuity rate published by the Financial Conduct Authority. On death the remaining pension fund can be used to provide pensions for dependants or paid to survivors as a lump sum, taxed at 35%.

From 6 April 2015, where the member dies before the age of 75, spouses or other beneficiaries who inherit joint life or guaranteed term annuities will no longer be taxed on the income. This aligns their treatment with dependant drawdown pensions.

it was also confirmed that drawdown pensions paid to spouses, or other dependants or nominees, would be tax-free where the member died before reaching the age of 75 and the pension first comes into payment on or after 6 April 2015. The fund can also be passed on tax-free as a lump sum, rather than potentially being subject to a 55% charge.

Not all dependant pensions will benefit from the tax exemption, however. Where the member dies before the age of 75 with either uncrystallised funds or a drawdown fund, if the beneficiary chooses to buy an annuity with the fund rather than go into drawdown, this will remain fully taxable. Similarly, there is no provision for making inherited scheme pensions (eg widow's pensions from final salary schemes) tax-free. Where the member dies after reaching the age of 75, all dependant pensions remain taxable, as they are under the current rules. Dependants who are already in receipt of annuities before 6 April 2015 will remain taxed on them in the same way as dependant drawdown pensions.

When a person reaches 75 years of age, they must opt for one of the following choices:

- Have a pension paid direct from an occupational scheme
- Use the pension fund to buy an annuity to provide a pension for the rest of life or
- Opt for an Alternatively Secured Pension or ASP. This is pension draw down but with the maximum income limited to 90% of the annuity rate for a 75 year old. On death, the remaining fund can be used to provide dependants pensions or, if there are no dependants, left to a charity or absorbed into the scheme to help other people's pensions. The person(s) whose pensions are to be enhanced can be nominated by the person whose pension it is.

We will be discussing options for taking pensions in more depth in Chapter 15

*****

Chapter 6

Choosing a Personal Pension Plan

There is a wide choice of personal pension schemes on offer. One common denominator is that the schemes are now heavily regulated by both the government and the Financial Conduct Authority. Most schemes will accept either a monthly contribution or a one-off lump sum payment per annum. The majority of schemes will allow a person to increase contributions. It is important to look for a plan that will allow a person to miss payments, in case of unemployment, sickness etc, without penalty.

Investments
Plans which allow individuals to choose their own investments are called' Self-invested Personal Pensions' (SIIPS) (see below). A person will build up their own fund of personal investments from a wide range of options such as shares, gilts, property and other areas. However, unless an individual has a large sum to invest, this is unlikely to be a wise bet. Pension companies can offer their own expertise and usually have far greater knowledge than the individual.

Self-invested Personal Pensions (SIPPs)
A self-invested personal pension (SIPP) is a pension 'wrapper' that holds investments until you retire and start to draw a retirement income. It is a type of personal pension and works in a similar way to a standard personal pension. The main

difference is that with a SIPP, you have more flexibility with the investments you can choose.

How it works

SIPPs aren't for everyone. Get advice if you're thinking about this type of personal pension. With standard personal pension schemes, your investments are managed for you within the pooled fund you have chosen. SIPPs are a form of personal pension that give you the freedom to choose and manage your own investments. Another option is to pay an authorised investment manager to make the decisions for you.

SIPPs are designed for people who want to manage their own fund by dealing with, and switching, their investments when they want to. SIPPs can also have higher charges than other personal pensions or stakeholder pensions. For these reasons, SIPPs tend to be more suitable for large funds and for people who are experienced in investing.

What you can and can't invest in

Most SIPPs allow you to select from a range of assets, such as:

- Unit trusts.
- Investment trusts.
- Government securities.
- Insurance company funds.
- Traded endowment policies.
- Some National Savings and Investment products.
- Deposit accounts with banks and building societies.
- Commercial property (such as offices, shops or factory premises).

- Individual stocks and shares quoted on a recognised UK or overseas stock exchange.

These aren't all of the investment options that are available – different SIPP providers offer different investment options. It's unlikely that you'll be able to invest directly in residential property within a SIPP. Residential property can't be held directly in a SIPP with the tax advantages that usually accompany pension investments. But, subject to some restrictions, including on personal use, residential property can be held in a SIPP through certain types of collective investments, such as real estate investment trusts, without losing the tax advantages.

How you access money in your SIPP
New rules introduced in April 2015 mean you can access and use your pension pot in any way you wish from age 55, (however, see below-accessing your pension funds to finance your business).

There's a lot to weigh up when working out which option or combination will provide you and any dependants with a reliable and tax-efficient income throughout your retirement. Be sure to use the free, government-backed Pension Wise service to help you understand your options or get financial advice.

Small Self-Administered Schemes (Ssas)
A SSAS is essentially an employer sponsored pension scheme with fewer than 12 people, where at least one member is connected with another, or with a trustee or the sponsoring

employer, and where some or all of the scheme assets are invested other than in insurance policies.

Every registered pension scheme is required to have a Scheme Administrator. If a Scheme Administrator is not appointed, then the Scheme trustees will normally become the Scheme Administrator by default. The Scheme Administrator must enrol online with HMRC before they can register the SSAS. Contributions to the SSAS must not be paid by either the employer or a member until the scheme has been registered with HM Revenue and Customs.

Any contributions, even if they are only paid to the Trustees' bank account, before the scheme is registered will not receive tax relief. The managing trustees must open a Scheme bank account. Contributions from the company (and the members) are paid into the bank account before they are invested at the managing trustees' discretion (subject to certain restrictions).

The structure of a Small Self-Administered Scheme could, for example, be as follows:

- Company and member payments
- Trustees' bank account
- Insurance Company investments

Self-administered part
– Commercial property eg. company premises.
– Loans to employer.
 –Deposit accounts.
– Open Ended Investment Companies (OEICs).
– Stock Exchange
– e.g. equities.
– Securities, etc

– e.g. gilts.

– Trustee Investment Bond.

There are clear benefits to holding assets under a registered pension scheme. For example, no capital gains tax liability arises when scheme assets are sold. On the other hand, when personally-held assets are sold this can trigger a Capital Gains Tax liability. A SSAS:

- Gives the managing trustees wide investment powers.
- Is a possible source of loan capital to the company for business expansion purposes, which may help minimise reliance on a third party (eg. bank).
- May be able to buy the company's premises – the SSAS managing trustees act as the landlord, meaning that the members retain control.
- Can be a possible source of equity capital for business expansion purposes which could avoid partial surrender of control to external interests.
- Is a vehicle for the managing trustees to back their investment judgement. A SSAS generally appeals to controlling directors who want
- To retain control over their pension benefits.
- To use the self-investment facility to help the company's development.
- A greater say in the way pension payments are invested

Releasing funds to finance business

One of the important points here is that, if the scheme is a small self-administered scheme it can be accessed to provide funds for a business, even if you are under the age of 55. This is known as 'pension-led funding'. Both SIIP's and SSAS's serve as an appropriate vehicle for this.

To effect pension-led funding you set up a sale and leaseback type arrangement whereby your pension buys assets from your business or loans money to your business secured against your retirement funds. However, it should be noted that there are advantages and disadvantages of doing this so you would need to talk the matter through with a pension provider with knowledge of this area. Scottish Widows is one such provider. There are many more. A reputable financial advisor will be able to point you in the right direction.

Fees and other charges

Those who invest your money on your behalf don't work for nothing. Fees are charged. The rate of interest offered will reflect the ultimate charge and there will probably be an administration fee too. Some plans have very complicated charging structures and it is very important that these are understood before decisions are made.

Other benefits from a personal pension

A personal pension scheme does not automatically offer a package of benefits in addition to the actual pension. Any additional benefits have to be paid for. The range of extra benefits includes lump sum life cover for dependants if death occurs before retirement, a pension for widow or widower or other partner, a waiver of contributions if there is an inability to work and a pension paid early if sickness or disability prevents working until retirement age.

A contracted out personal pension must allow for a widow's or widower's pension to be payable if the widow or widower is over 45 years of age, or is younger than 45 but qualifies for child benefit. The pension would be whatever amount can be bought by the fund built up through investing the contracting-out rebates. The widow or widower has an open market option, which gives him or her a right to shop around for a different pension provider rather than remain with the existing provider.

The pension could cease if the widow or widower remarries while under the state pension age, or ceases to be eligible for child benefit whilst still under 45. This depends on the terms of the contract at the time of death.

A contracted out widow's or widower's pension built up before 6th April 1997 must be increased each year in line with inflation, up to a maximum of 3% a year. For post April 1997 pensions this must be up to 5% per year and after 6th April 2005, pensions taken out don't have to increase at all.

With the exception of contracted out plans, a person must choose at the time of taking out the plan which death benefits to have as part of the scheme. Broadly, they should be in line with the benefits mentioned above.

Retirement due to ill-health

If a person has to retire due to ill-health, a pension can be taken from a personal plan at any age. However, a person's inability to work must be clearly demonstrated and backed up with a professional opinion.

Taking a pension early will result in a reduced pension because what is in the pot will be less. However, there are ways of mitigating this, one way to ensure that a waiver of premiums in the event of sickness is included in the pension. In this way the plan will continue to grow even though a person is ill. Another way is to take out permanent disability insurance. This insurance will guarantee that the pension that you will get when you cannot work will at least be a minimum amount.

The Pension Protection Fund

Members of defined benefit occupational pension schemes are protected through the PPF, which will pay regular compensation, based on your pension amount, if the company becomes insolvent and the pension scheme doesn't have enough money to pay your pension. The PPF applies to most defined benefit schemes where the employer became insolvent after 6th April 2005. You should check with the PPF about levels of compensation.

The Financial Assistance Scheme

If you are an individual scheme member and have lost out on your pension as a result of your scheme winding up after 1st January 1997 and the introduction of PPF you may be able to get financial help from the FAS, which is administered by the Pension Protection Fund, if:

- your defined benefit scheme was under funded and
- your employer is insolvent, no longer exists or has entered into a valid compromise agreement with the trustees of the pension fund to avoid insolvency; or
- in some circumstances, your final salary scheme was wound up because it could not pay members benefits even if the employer continues trading.

In the case of fraud or theft

If the shortfall in your company pension scheme was due to Fraud or theft, it may be possible to recover some of the money through the PPF who operate what is known as the Fraud Compensation Scheme.

The Pension Tracing Service

If you think that you may have an old pension but are not sure of the details, the Pension Tracing Service, part of the Pension Service, may be able to help. They can be contacted on 0800 1223 170 (general enquiries) and will give you full details of their scheme and also will tell you what they need from you in order to trace the pension. www.pensiontracingservice.com.

****

Chapter 7

Job Related (Occupational) Pensions

The best way to save for retirement is through an occupational pension scheme. Employers will also contribute and pay administration costs. Schemes normally provide an additional package of benefits such as protection if you become disabled, protection for dependants and protection against inflation.

Some pension schemes are related to final salary and provide a pension that equates to a proportion of salary. However, it must be said that a lot of these schemes have wound down due to the difficulty of providing retirement benefits in these straitened times..

Limits on your pension savings
These limits apply collectively to all private pensions (occupational schemes and personal pensions) that you may have)

See overleaf.

Type of limit	Description	Amount
Annual contribution limit	The maximum contributions on which you can get tax relief. You can continue contributing to your 75th birthday	£3,600 or 100% of your UK relevant earnings for the year whichever is the greater
Annual allowance	The maximum addition to your pension savings in any one year (including for example employers contributions). Anything above the limit normally triggers a tax charge, but this does not apply in the year that you start to draw the pension.	Tax year 2019/20 £40,000
Lifetime allowance	The cumulative value of benefits that can be drawn from your pension savings. Any amount drawn that exceeds the limits triggers a tax charge.	Tax year 2019/20 £1,030,000million

Tax advantages of occupational schemes

The tax advantages of occupational schemes are:

- A person receives tax relief on the amount that he or she pays into the scheme
- Employers contributions count as a tax-free benefit

- Capital gains on the contributions build up tax free
- At retirement part of the pension fund can be taken as a tax-free lump sum. The rest is taken as a taxable pension

Qualifying to join an occupational scheme

An occupational scheme can be either open to all or restricted to certain groups, i.e. different schemes for different groups. Schemes are not allowed to discriminate in terms of race or gender or any other criteria. Employees do not have to join a scheme and can leave when they wish. There might however be restrictions on rejoining or joining a scheme later on.

Not all employers offer an occupational scheme. Another pension arrangement such as a stakeholder scheme or Group Pension Scheme might be offered. However, note that Auto Enrolment is now in force.

Automatic enrolment

To help more people save for their retirement, the government has made major changes to how workplace pensions operate. In the past, it was up to workers to decide whether they wanted to join their employer's pension scheme. But now, all employers will have to automatically enrol their eligible workers into a workplace pension scheme unless the worker chooses to opt out. As a result, many more people will be able to build up savings to provide them with an income when they choose to stop working.

When did automatic enrolment start?

Automatic enrolment was introduced in stages since 2012. The largest employers started first, followed by medium-sized and then small employers. All employers, including new employers, should now be part of automatic enrolment.

Who will be automatically enrolled?

Whether you work full time or part time, your employer will have to enrol you in a workplace pension scheme if you:

- work in the UK
- are not already in a suitable workplace pension scheme
- are at least 22 years old, but under State Pension age
- earn more than £10,000 a year for the tax year 2018-19.

As long as you meet these criteria you'll also be covered if you're on a short-term contract, an agency pays your wages, or you're away on maternity, adoption or carer's leave.

If you earn less than £10,000, but above £6,032 (for the tax year 2018-19) your employer doesn't have to automatically enrol you in the scheme.

However, you can still ask to join, in which case your employer can't refuse and must make contributions for you.

How much will I have to contribute?

There is a minimum total amount that has to be contributed by you, your employer, and the government in the form of tax relief. From April 2018 these minimums increased to 3% from you and 2% from your employer. In April 2019 the minimum will increase again to 5% from you and 3% from your employer.

The minimum contribution applies to anything you earn over £6,032 up to a limit of £46,350 (in the tax year 2018-19). This slice of your earnings is known as "qualifying earnings".

So, if you were earning £18,000 a year, your contribution would be a percentage of £11,968 (the difference between £6,032 and £18,000).

Some employers apply the minimum pension contribution to the whole of your earnings, not just to qualifying earnings. This depends on how they have set up the scheme. If you are not sure whether you pay pension contributions on qualifying earnings or on full earnings, talk to your employer.

Your employer will let you know how much of your earnings you'll need to contribute. They might tell you this as a sum of money or as a percentage.

Increases in the minimum contribution

The total minimum contribution is currently set at 5% of your earnings. This is made up of 3% from you, which includes tax relief, and 2% from your employer. From April 2019, this will increase to 8% of your earnings. That's 5% from you, which includes tax relief, and 3% from your employer.

Automatic enrolment when you have more than one job

If you have more than one job, each job is treated separately for automatic enrolment purposes. This means some jobs will sign you up to pay into a pension automatically, while others won't.

Each of your employers will check whether you're eligible to join their pension scheme. If you are, then you'll be automatically enrolled in that employer's workplace pension scheme.

If you don't want to be a member of more than one scheme you can choose to opt out of one of them, but you don't have to. You can pay into more than one pension scheme if you want to. If you earn more than £6,032 but less than £10,000 in any of your jobs you won't be automatically enrolled in that employer's pension scheme, but you can ask to join. If you do, your employer also has to contribute. If you earn less than £6,032 a year in any of your jobs you can still ask to join that employer's pension scheme, but your employer doesn't have to contribute.

Do I have any choice about being enrolled?

You can opt out of your employer's workplace pension scheme after you've been enrolled. But if you do, you'll lose out on your employer's contribution to your pension, as well as the government's contribution in the form of tax relief. If you decide to opt out, ask the people who run your employer's workplace pension scheme for an opt-out form. You must then return your completed form to your employer, not to the people who run the scheme. If you decide to opt out within a month of being enrolled, any payments you've made into your pension pot during this time will be refunded to you.

After the first month, you can still opt out at any time, but any payments you've made will stay in your pension pot for retirement rather than be refunded. You can re-join your employer's workplace pension scheme at a later date if you want to. By law, your employer must re-enrol you back into the scheme approximately every three years, as long as you still meet the eligibility criteria.

Should I stay in or opt out?

For most people, staying in a workplace pension is a good idea, particularly as your employer must contribute to it. The contribution your employer makes to your pension is part of your overall employment package – so opting out is like turning down pay. This makes workplace pensions a great way to save for retirement. However, there are circumstances in which it might not make sense to stay in. For example, if you're dealing with unmanageable debt

Choosing a pension scheme

Employers with an automatic enrolment duty will need to choose a pension scheme they can use for automatic enrolment. Information from the Pensions Regulator will be available to help inform this decision. Employers might use an existing scheme or set up a new one with a pension provider. In addition, there is the National Employment Savings Trust (NEST). NEST is a pension scheme with the following characteristics:

- It has a public service obligation, meaning it must accept all employers who apply.

It has been established by government to ensure that employers, including those that employ low to medium earners, can access pension savings and comply with their automatic enrolment duties.

Whether the scheme an employer uses for automatic enrolment is new or not, it must meet certain specific set out in legislation. The scheme cannot:

- Impose barriers, such as probationary periods or age limits for workers.
- Require staff to make an active choice to join or take other action, e.g. having to sign a form or provide extra information to the scheme themselves, either prior to joining or to retain active membership of the scheme.

Each pension scheme will have its own rules, but all employers will need to provide the scheme with certain information about the person who is automatically enrolled. process called 'certification'.

More information is available from the Pensions Regulator at www.thepensionsregulator.gov.uk.

Pension entitlements

The amount of pension that a person receives from an occupational scheme will depend in part on the type of scheme that it is. Currently, there are two main types:

- Defined benefit schemes, promising a given level of benefit on retirement, usually final salary schemes
- Money purchase schemes (defined contribution schemes), where a person builds up their own savings pot. There are hybrid schemes where both the above are on offer but these are not common.

Final salary schemes

With final salary schemes, a person is promised (but not guaranteed) a certain level of pension and other benefits related to earnings. This is independent of what is paid into the scheme. Final salary schemes work well when a person

82

stays with their employer for a long length of time or work in the public sector.

A person in such a scheme will typically pay around 5% of their salary into the scheme with the employer paying the balance of the cost which will be around 10% of salary on average. When the stock market is doing well the employer is safeguarded but when the economic climate is changing, such as at this point in time then the story is somewhat different and the employer has to pay more to maintain the level of pension. This is why such pension schemes are being withdrawn.

The pension received at retirement is based on a formula and related to final salary and years of membership in the scheme. The maximum usually builds up over 40 years. The accrual rate in such a scheme is one sixtieth or one eightieth of salary per year in the scheme.

If a person leaves the pension scheme before retirement they are still entitled to receive a pension from the scheme, based on contributions.

Money purchase schemes

Money purchase pension schemes are like any other forms of savings or investment. Money is paid in and grows in value and the proceeds eventually provide a pension. The scheme is straightforward and has its upsides and downsides. The upside is that it is simple and portable. The downside is that it is related to the growth of the economy and can shrink as well as grow.

It is more difficult to plan for retirement with this kind of scheme, as distinct from the final salary scheme. As we have seen, employers prefer this kind of scheme because, although they pay into it, it doesn't place any onerous responsibilities on them.

The pension that is received on retirement will depend on the amount paid into the scheme, charges deducted for management of the scheme, how well the investment grows and the rate, called the annuity rate, at which the fund can be converted into pension. A major problem for pension schemes has been the decline in annuity rates in recent years. With most money purchase schemes the proceeds are usually given to an insurer who will administer the funds. The trustees of the scheme will choose the insurer, in most cases. In some cases, contributors are given the choice of investment. This choice will usually include:

- A with-profits basis which is a medium-risk option and which is safer and more likely to provide a good return if a person remains with the same employer. The value of the fund cannot fall and will grow steadily as reversionary bonuses are added. On retirement a person will receive a terminal bonus, which represents a chunk of the overall return
- A unit linked fund- where money is invested in one or more funds, e.g. shares, property, gilts and so on.

The cash balance scheme

A cash balance scheme lies somewhere between a final salary scheme and a money purchase scheme. Whereas in a final salary scheme a person is promised a certain level of pension at retirement with a cash balance scheme a person is promised a certain amount of money with which to buy a pension. The amount of cash can be expressed in a number of ways, for example as a percentage of salary per annum for each year of membership. So if a person is earning £50,000 per annum and the cash balance scheme is promising 15% of salary for each year of membership, there would be a pension fund of £50,000 times 15% which equals £75,000 after 10 years of membership.

Tax

Whichever type of pension that is offered, the government sets limits on maximum amounts that a person can receive. HMRC sets limits on occupational schemes which relate mainly to final salary schemes and which are shown below. More information about tax liabilities and occupational pensions can be found at:

www.gov.uk/government/organisations/hm-revenue-customs

Contributions into occupational schemes

Some occupational schemes are non-contributory, which means that the employer pays all contributions. The majority of schemes, however, are contributory, with the employer and employee contributing. Usually, the employee will pay 5% of salary. With money purchase schemes the employer will also pay a specified amount of salary. With final salary schemes, which as stated are becoming less and less common, the employer will make up the balance needed to provide the specified amount. Both employer and employee will get tax relief on contributions.

Top-up schemes exist which can be used to top up pension pots but these are liable for tax in the usual way. There are two main types of top-up scheme:

- Unfunded schemes. With these schemes, an employer simply pays benefits at the time that a person reaches retirement. Income tax will be due on any benefits, even on lump sums
- funded schemes (Funded Unapproved Retirement Benefit Schemes or FURBS). This is where the employer pays contributions which build up funds to provide the eventual benefits. At the time that contributions are made they count as tax-liable fringe benefits. Usually the fund is arranged as a trust, which attracts only normal rates of tax. The benefits are tax-free when they are paid out, having been subject to tax.

If an employer runs a scheme which a person is eligible to join they must be given information about it automatically. The rules are as follows:

- an explanatory booklet must be given within two months of commencing employment if eligible to join, or within 13 weeks of joining
- each year a summary trustees report an annual accounts must be given
- employees can request a copy of the full accounts which must be provided on request
- an annual benefit statement must be provided
- options on leaving the scheme and benefit entitlements, transfer value must be provided within 3 months of request
- any announcements of changes to the scheme must be given to the scheme member within one month of the change being made

Contracting Out Through Occupational Schemes

iIn addition to the basic state pension, the state previously provided a second-tier top-up pension, based on how much you earned. Introduced in 1978 and originally called the State Earnings Related Pension Scheme (Serps), it became State Second Pension (S2P) in 2002. Before 2012's rule changes, employees were allowed to 'contract out' of this additional pension. In exchange for lower National Insurance contributions, they gave up part or all of it and received extra pension from their occupational scheme or personal/stakeholder pension instead.

Until 1988, people could only contract out if they were members of a defined benefit (DB) occupational pension scheme. In 1988, the government extended this to defined contribution (DC) or money purchase occupational schemes and personal pensions. It gave incentives to encourage people to leave the state earnings-related pension scheme (Serps). For the first five years of the scheme, the government paid an extra 2% of your earnings into your personal pension. By 1992, more than 5 million people had left Serps for a personal pension.

Rule changes for contracting out-defined benefit pension scheme

If you've been in a contracted-out defined benefit (DB) scheme, you and your employer have paid a slightly lower National Insurance (NI) contribution. This reflects the fact that neither of you have contributed to the state additional pension. From April 2012, only those in a defined benefit (DB) scheme have been contracted out and paid a lower rate.

Those in a defined contribution (DC) scheme were contracted back in and paid National Insurance at the full rate. They accumulated state second pension (S2P) between 2012 and 2016.

Contracting out on a DB basis ended in April 2016, when the government's state pension reforms came into force. People qualifying for the state pension before 6 April 2016 will get less additional state pension if they've spent time contracted out, and those qualifying on or after 6 April 2016 will get a lower 'starting amount'.

****

Chapter 8

Group Personal Pension Schemes

What is a group personal pension?

Group personal pensions (GPPs) are a type of defined contribution pension which some employers offer to their workers. As with other types of defined-contribution scheme, members in a GPP build up a personal pension pot, which they then convert into an income at retirement.

As stated earlier, In a group personal pension, the scheme is run by a pension provider that your employer chooses, but your pension is an individual contract between you and the provider. The provider claims tax relief at the basic rate on your contributions and adds it to your fund. If you're a higher or additional-rate taxpayer, you'll need to claim the additional rebate through your tax return.

Your pension pot builds up using your contributions, any contributions your employer makes, investment returns and tax relief.

How your pension grows while you are working

The fund is usually invested in stocks and shares, along with other investments, with the aim of growing the fund over the years before you retire. You can usually choose from a range of funds to invest in. Remember though that the value of investments might go up or down. You can access and use your pension pot in any way you wish from age 55.

You can:

- Take a quarter of your pot as a tax-free lump sum and then convert some or all of the rest into a taxable retirement income (known as an annuity).

- Take your whole pension pot as a lump sum in one go. A quarter (25%) will be tax free and the rest will be subject to tax at your normal tax rate. Bear in mind that a large lump sum could tip you into a higher tax bracket for the year.

- Take lump sums as and when you need them. A quarter of each lump sum will be tax free and the rest will be subject to tax at your normal tax rate. Bear in mind that a large lump sum could tip you into a higher tax bracket for the year.

- Take a quarter of your pension pot (or of the amount you allocate for drawdown) as a tax-free lump sum, then use the rest to provide a regular taxable income.

The size of your pension pot and amount of income you get when you retire will depend on:

- How long you save for
- How much you pay into the fund
- How much you take as a cash lump sum(s)
- How well your investments have performed
- How much, if anything, your employer pays in
- What charges have been taken out of your fund by your pension provider

When you retire, your pension provider will usually offer you a retirement income (an annuity) based on your pot size, but you don't have to take this and it isn't your only option.

If you're unsure about your options and how they work, you can get free and impartial guidance from Pension Wise, a service run by The Pensions Advisory Service and Citizens Advice. You can find FCA registered financial advisers who specialise in retirement planning by going to pensionwise.gov.uk

What you need to think about

Some employers will also contribute to the workplace pension they run, meaning you'll lose out on their contributions if you decide not to join. Unless your priority is dealing with unmanageable debt or you really can't afford it you should consider joining one of these schemes if you can. The amount your employer puts in can depend on how much you're willing to save, and might increase as you get older. For example your employer might be prepared to match your contribution on a like-for-like basis up to a certain level, but could be more generous.

Changing jobs

If you change jobs, your group personal pension is usually automatically converted into a personal pension and you can continue paying into it independently. However, you should check to see if your new employer offers a pension scheme. You might find you'll be better off joining your new employer's scheme, especially if the employer contributes.

Compare the benefits available through your employer's scheme with your group personal pension. If you decide to stop paying into a group personal pension, you can leave the pension fund to carry on growing through investment growth. Check to see if there are extra charges for doing this.

****

Chapter 9

Stakeholder Pension Schemes

About stakeholder pensions

With the introduction of automatic enrolment, the requirement for an employer to provide access for staff to a stakeholder pension scheme has been removed to avoid employers being subject to overlapping duties. Stakeholder pensions are a type of flexible pension arrangement introduced in 2001 designed for individuals without access to employer sponsored pension arrangements, such as the self-employed. Individuals may take out stakeholder pensions individually or through their employer. Stakeholder pensions must satisfy a number of minimum conditions which are described below.

Stakeholder pensions defined

The legal requirements for stakeholder pensions are included in the Welfare Reform and Pensions Act 1999 and underlying legislation. To qualify as a stakeholder pension, a pension scheme must satisfy a number of minimum conditions:

- it must be a defined contribution arrangement;
- management charges in each year must not amount to more than 1.5% of the total value of the fund (and are taken from the fund) for each year until the 10th year

of continuous membership in the scheme when the cap reduces to 1%;

- as well as the 1.5%, the law allows pension providers to recover costs and charges they have to pay for certain other things. For example, when they have to pay any stamp duty or other charges for buying and selling investments for the fund , or for particular circumstances such as the costs of sharing a pension when a couple divorce. These expenses are found in other pension schemes not just stakeholder pensions;

- any extra services and any extra charges not provided for by law must be optional. Extra services must be offered under a separate arrangement with clearly defined costs for the services being offered;

- the scheme must accept transfers in, and there must be no additional charges for this or for transferring to a different stakeholder pension;

- the minimum contribution to a stakeholder pension cannot be set higher than £20 (schemes may set a lower minimum contribution if they wish). Contributions can be paid weekly, monthly (or at other intervals), or they can be a single one-off contribution;

- to look after the interests of their members, schemes must have either trustees or stakeholder managers;

- for trust-based schemes, a third of the trustees must be independent;

- schemes must appoint a scheme auditor or a reporting accountant to check the annual declaration made by the trustees or managers to ensure that the scheme complies with the charging regulations;

- schemes must have a statement of investment principles;

- schemes must have a default investment option which is subject to lifestyling (this means that during the years leading up to retirement a member's pension is gradually moved into investments that are considered to be less volatile with the aim of providing greater security as they approach retirement).

Who should take out a stakeholder pension?

Stakeholder pensions are available to almost everybody, including people in employment, fixed contract staff, the self-employed and people who are not actually working but can afford to make contributions. It's also possible to contribute to someone else's stakeholder pension - for instance someone can make contributions to their non-working partner's stakeholder scheme on their behalf.

How much can be invested in a stakeholder pension?

There is no limit to the amount that can be invested in a stakeholder pension scheme. However, tax relief can only be obtained on contributions up to a maximum annual contribution limit (known as an individual's 'annual allowance'). For the tax year 2018/19, this is set at the lower of 100% of an individual's UK earnings or £40,000 – carry forward of unused allowances may be permitted in some circumstances. It is possible to contribute up to £3,600 per year (including tax relief) into a stakeholder pension scheme even if a person is not earning.

A member of an occupational pension scheme may also contribute to a stakeholder pension scheme.

Trust schemes and non-trust schemes

Stakeholder pension schemes can be set up under a trust (where a body of trustees is responsible for managing the scheme) or can be set up by deed poll. Where the scheme is set up by deed poll, the manager of the scheme (the 'stakeholder manager') may enter into contracts with each member of the scheme or a person acting on their behalf. The stakeholder manager could be an insurance company, bank, building society and must be authorised by the Financial Conduct Authority (FCA) to carry out stakeholder business.

Stakeholder schemes must be registered with The Pensions Regulator. The regulator is responsible for enforcing the conditions that define a stakeholder pension and allow it to be registered. The regulator can fine trustees and providers for falling short of the conditions. In extreme cases it can withdraw stakeholder registration and order the winding-up of the scheme.

Financial Conduct Authority (FCA)

The FCA will regulate the marketing and promotion of all schemes that are set up as stakeholder pension schemes.

Financial advice on stakeholder pensions

Any extra charges for provision of advice on stakeholder pensions must be entirely optional. Any charge levied for advice over and above the 1.5% stakeholder charges limit should be entirely separate from the scheme charging structure. Financial advisers must keep to the rules laid down by the FCA and must state which organisation regulates their work. The Pensions Regulator and the FCA will liaise closely, to ensure that stakeholder schemes are run according to the rules.

Tax and national insurance
Tax relief

Normally there will be tax relief on any payments into a stakeholder pension up to an individual's annual allowance limit as described above. HM Revenue and Customs (HMRC) will send the amount direct to the trustees or stakeholder pension scheme manager.

Personal contributions paid to a stakeholder pension scheme are made net of basic rate tax (i.e. 20%). People who pay income tax at the higher rate (40%) may be able to claim back the tax difference from HMRC at the end of the tax year through self-assessment or by contacting HMRC. Individuals who are additional rate-tax payers may be able to claim additional tax relief at their highest rate, up to a maximum of 30%, through self-assessment.

Regular information for members

Once someone has joined a stakeholder pension scheme, the trustees or stakeholder manager must provide them with regular information. This information will include an annual statement detailing how much has been paid in and how the individual's fund is progressing. It may include a forecast of the likely pension on retirement.

Existing employer stakeholder schemes

Employers must continue to deduct and pay the contributions for existing stakeholder schemes to the pension provider. This will continue to apply until the employee concerned stops paying contributions into their stakeholder pension.

Automatic enrolment and stakeholder pensions

Stakeholder pension schemes can be used by employers for automatic-enrolment purposes provided the schemes meet the necessary criteria. All employers will be required to meet their pension automatic enrolment obligations, although not at the same time. Larger employers started from 1 October 2012 but each employer will have a 'staging date' by which they must comply with the regulations. There will be a period between 1 October 2012 and when an employer reaches its staging date where some employees will not have an opportunity to join a work based pension scheme. However, those individuals who wish to enrol voluntarily in a stakeholder pension scheme will still be able to do so, albeit not necessarily through a scheme set up by their employer. The stakeholder pensions register on the regulator's website gives the details of the choice of stakeholder pensions available.

Contributions to stakeholder pension employer schemes

Employers must pay employee contributions to schemes within a specified timescale, and the regulator will be responsible for dealing with any reports of late payment of contributions by employers. If a stakeholder manager or trustee does not receive the expected amount from the employer on the date it is due, they have a statutory duty to report the matter to the regulator. The regulator will monitor reports of late payments and will take appropriate action against the employer where necessary.

Monitoring by scheme managers or trustees

Stakeholder managers or trustees are required to monitor that payments made by the employer or deducted from employees' pay are for the correct amount and are paid in on time. Employers need to maintain payment records and inform the trustees or stakeholder manager of any changes. Trustees must report a material payment failures to the regulator and members within a reasonable period where there is 'reasonable cause to believe' that this failure is likely to be of material significance to the regulator in the exercise of its functions. The regulator will then consider whether or not to take action.

******

Chapter 10

Leaving an Occupational Scheme

There are a number of reasons why people may want to leave an occupational scheme before retirement. One of the main ones is leaving an employer to take up another job. It could be that there is a desire to leave one pension scheme and enter another. Whatever the reason, there are a number of questions that need answering.

If a person leaves an occupational pension fund and has been a member of it for two years or more that scheme must provide a pension at retirement, called a deferred pension, or allow transfer of the contributions. A new pension scheme is not legally obliged to accept transfer.

Obtaining a refund of contributions

If you leave your pension scheme, you do not lose the benefits you have built up. They continue to belong to you and you have several options for what to do with them. Your scheme administrator or pension provider should tell you which options apply to you.

If you leave your defined benefit or money purchase pension scheme having been a member for less than two years, you may be able to take a refund of the contributions that you've paid, if the scheme's rules permit this.

As of 1 October 2015, members of occupational defined contribution pension schemes will no longer be entitled to short-service refunds if they leave employment (or opt out) with less than two years qualifying service.

The change only applies to individuals who became members of an occupational pension scheme on or after 1 October 2015, or who re-joined an arrangement having already taken a refund or transferred out. Those with less than 30 days service will still be able to request a short service refund of just their contributions.

If you have made any contributions using a salary sacrifice arrangement, these cannot be refunded as they are classed as employer contributions and must remain in your pension pot.

If you have been a member of a personal pension or stakeholder pension scheme, you only have the option of taking a refund if you've been a member for less than thirty days, and you haven't made any contributions using a salary sacrifice arrangement.

In each case, the amount that you receive will have been subject to tax to take account of any tax relief you received when you paid contributions.

Contributions refunded from a defined benefit or money purchase pension scheme are taxed at 20% on the first £20,000 and at 50% on the remainder.

The amount you receive back from a personal pension or stakeholder pension scheme is the contributions that you paid net of basic rate income tax relief.

*****

Chapter 11

Transferring Pension Rights

Transferring your pension

Leaving your pension scheme occurs when, for example you leave your employer, if you decide to opt out or stop making contributions. If you leave your pension scheme, the benefits you've built up still belong to you. You normally have the option to leave them where they are or to transfer them to another pension scheme.

If you leave your pension scheme, you do not lose the benefits you have built up. They continue to belong to you and you have several options for what to do with them. Your scheme administrator or pension provider should tell you which options apply to you.

Most schemes will allow you to transfer your pension pot to another pension scheme, which could be a new employer's workplace pension scheme, a personal pension scheme, a self-invested personal pension (SIPP) or a stakeholder pension (SHP) scheme.

You don't have to decide straight away – you can generally transfer at any time up a year before the date that you are expected to start drawing retirement benefits. In some cases, it's also possible to transfer to a new pension provider after you have started to draw retirement benefits.

UK transfers

If you leave your pension scheme the benefits you've built up still belong to you. One of the options that you have is to transfer them to another pension scheme.

Transferring to another UK pension scheme

You can normally transfer pension benefits held in a scheme that you have left to a new pension scheme at any time up to, generally, one year before the date when you are expected to start taking retirement benefits. In some circumstances, you can also transfer after you have started to receive retirement benefits but this is not common.

The first step is to find out your cash equivalent transfer value (CETV), also known as the transfer value, by asking your scheme administrator or pension provider. They may ask you to do this in writing, and may have a form that you need to complete.

Your scheme administrator or pension provider will then provide you with a Statement of Entitlement. If you're eligible for a CETV this must be provided within three months of you asking for a transfer value. It's a written document that sets out your transfer value, together with details of the benefits you have built up under the scheme, and information that your new scheme will need if you decide to proceed with the transfer. There may also be additional forms included to start the transfer process.

If your Statement of Entitlement relates to benefits held in a defined benefit pension scheme, the transfer value is guaranteed for three months*. If you do not start the transfer process within the three month period, the actual amount transferred may be higher or lower than the amount shown in the Statement of Entitlement.

If you're a member of a defined contribution pension scheme, the transfer value may change as the value of the investments held in your scheme changes.

If you decide to transfer to a new scheme, your scheme administrator or pension provider must pay the benefits across to the new scheme within six months from the start of the transfer process.

Unfunded defined benefit pension scheme

If you're a member of an unfunded defined benefit pension scheme (public sector pension schemes), you will not be able to transfer to a defined contribution pension scheme after 5 April 2015, but you will still be able to transfer to another defined benefit pension scheme.

If you're a member of a funded defined benefit pension scheme (usually a private sector defined benefit scheme), you are able to transfer to a new defined benefit or defined contribution pension scheme, but, if you are transferring to a defined contribution pension scheme after 5 April 2015, you will be required to take advice before the transfer can proceed if the value of the benefits is £30,000 or more. You will have to pay for this advice.

What happens when your pension has been transferred

Once you have transferred to a new scheme, you'll have given up all benefits under the old scheme. If you are transferring from a defined benefit pension scheme, this may mean that you have given up some valuable, guaranteed pension benefits, so it is a good idea to seek regulated financial advice to check that a transfer is in your best interests.

If you are transferring to a defined contribution scheme, you should check the charges that may apply under the new scheme.

Overseas transfers

If you leave your pension scheme the benefits you've built up still belong to you. You have the option to transfer them to another pension scheme, which could be based abroad.

If you're living or working overseas and you have pension benefits held in one or more UK pension schemes, you may want to think about transferring these to an overseas pension scheme (which could include your current employer's scheme).

UK pension benefits can only be transferred to an overseas pension scheme if it is recognised by HM Revenue & Customs as a qualifying recognised overseas pension scheme (QROPS).

To be recognised as a QROPS, the scheme must be:

- Regulated as a pension scheme in the country where it is established; and
- Recognised for tax purposes (so benefits that are paid to you from the scheme must be subject to taxation).

If the new scheme is not a QROPS, your scheme administrator or pension provider can't transfer your UK pension benefits to it. If it's a QROPS, the transfer goes ahead in the same way as a transfer to a UK pension scheme. If the new scheme is not currently a QROPS, it can apply to be approved as a QROPS and, if this is granted, the transfer can go ahead. If your UK pension benefits that you are transferring include contracted-out benefits, your UK scheme will have to go through a few extra steps to make sure that the QROPS you are transferring to is suitable.

Transfer incentives and pension increase exchange

Your employer may use transfer incentives and pension increase exchange exercises to try to reduce the running costs of their defined benefit or CARE pension scheme.

Transfer incentives

If you have left your defined benefit or CARE workplace pension scheme, your employer may offer to increase the transfer value to encourage you to transfer your built-up pension benefits to a new pension scheme.

You may also be offered a similar incentive as an active member of a scheme, if you agree to transfer your benefits to a new scheme.

In each case, your employer is looking to reduce the running costs of their workplace pension scheme by moving future liabilities (your future pension benefits) out of the scheme.

If your employer offers you a transfer incentive, they are expected to follow a code of conduct to ensure that you are able to make an informed decision about what is best for you, without being pressured by your employer to transfer. A key element of the code of conduct is that your employer should offer you access to regulated financial advice, paid for by your employer, to help you decide whether to transfer your pension benefits to a new scheme.

Pension increase exchange (PIE) exercises

If you're receiving a pension from your pension scheme, or are about to start receiving it, your employer may offer a one-off increase to the amount that you are receiving as a pension in return for you giving up your right to receive the annual pension increases that are set out in the scheme rules. If you accept the PIE, your pension will be paid at the new, higher rate for the rest of your life, but without any future annual increases.

Over time, this means that the purchasing power of your pension income may be eroded by the effects of inflation.

Your employer doesn't have to offer you access to regulated financial advice provided that the PIE you are offered meets certain minimum standards set out in the code of practice and you are offered some guidance.

The Pension Regulator has set out five key principles that it expects to be followed in any transfer incentive or PIE exercise. These are set out, with further information, in a statement called "Incentive Exercises", which you can read here. The Pension Regulator will investigate cases where it receives reports that the key principles have not been followed.

You should obtain all necessary information and consider the long-term implications of transfer incentives or pension increase exchange very carefully before you decide to accept an offer. If you are offered regulated financial advice, this could help you to reach the right decision.

Things to think about

Before you transfer pension benefits, there are a number of different things you should think about.

The decision about whether or not to transfer benefits is not always easy. In some cases you may want to seek advice from a regulated financial adviser. Here are some of the things that you may want to consider.

Transferring from a defined benefits pension scheme
When you transfer benefits from a defined benefits pension scheme, you are not transferring the actual benefits but a cash amount, the cash equivalent transfer value (CETV). When the CETV is transferred, you give up all of your benefits in the old scheme.

If you transfer to a new defined benefits scheme, the CETV is used to buy pension benefits in the scheme. These are unlikely to be the same as the benefits you had in the old scheme and you will be subject to the new scheme's rules. It is rare that defined benefit schemes will accept a transfer into it except in the public sector.

If you transfer to a defined contribution pension scheme, the CETV is added to your pension pot and is invested in the funds that you select. Its value when you start to draw retirement benefits will depend on the amount of the CETV, how long it has been invested, investment growth over this period and the level of any charges.

It's worth remembering that defined benefits pension schemes give a guaranteed level of pension income, whereas the benefits under a defined contribution pension scheme depend on investment performance during the time that the money is invested. If you transfer from a defined benefit scheme to a defined contribution scheme, the retirement benefits you receive may be higher or lower than the benefits you would have received if you had stayed in the defined benefit scheme. You should certainly consider seeking advice for these types of transfer.

As of April 2015, it is a requirement to get advice before transferring from a defined benefit to a defined contribution scheme if the value of your benefits is over £30,000. In addition, transfers from unfunded public sector schemes to defined contribution schemes are no longer available.

If you are transferring from a defined contribution pension scheme, you will usually be transferring to another defined contribution scheme. The amount available to transfer to the new scheme is usually based on the value of your pension pot, although there may be charges for transferring. When the transfer is completed, the value of your pension pot in your new scheme will be its value before the transfer plus the amount transferred.

You will need to choose how to invest the money transferred into the new scheme so before transferring it's worth considering where you would like to invest and what choices are available in the new scheme. It's unlikely that the new scheme will offer the same investment options as your old scheme. You should also check the level of charges that may be payable.

If you are able to transfer to a defined benefits pension scheme, the new scheme's administrator will be able to tell you the additional benefits the scheme will give you in return for the transfer value.

Moving abroad

You're now allowed to be a member of a UK registered pension scheme regardless of where you live or where your employer is based. If you move abroad you have several options with your pension to consider:

Option 1 – leave your pensions in the UK pension plan.
Your pension will continue to be held by your pension provider until you claim it. You can request early payment of these pensions from age 55 at which point you may be able to take up to 25% of the value as a lump sum and use the remained to provide a pension for your lifetime.
Anybody who has a defined contribution pension scheme will be permitted to access their pension pots as cash from the age of 55.

If you are not able, or do not draw your pension, at age 55 you can claim your pension from your normal pension date. If you decide on this option it would be worth asking for regular updates of your pension if this is not automatically provided.

Option 2 – transfer your UK pensions to an approved arrangement in your new country of residence.
It may be possible to transfer your UK pensions to a pension arrangement overseas if the pension plan is a Qualifying Recognised Overseas Pension Scheme (QROPS). In order to qualify as a QROPS and in order to transfer to a QROPS certain conditions must be met.

Option 3 - Paying into a UK pension scheme from abroad
Living abroad, or working for an employer who is based overseas, no longer limits the amount either of you can pay into a UK pension scheme. The downside is that tax relief may be limited - or not available at all.

Do you qualify for tax relief?

To get tax relief on your contributions, you must have been a relevant UK individual for the tax year in question. This means:

- you had relevant UK earnings chargeable to UK income tax during that tax year
- you were tax resident in the UK at some time during that tax year;
- you were tax resident in the UK:
- at some time during the previous five tax years; and
- when you joined the pension scheme;

for that tax year, you or your spouse or civil partner has general earnings from Crown employment (i.e. working abroad for the UK Government for a long period) which were subject to UK tax

Tax relief limits

Tax relief on your contributions is limited to whichever is the greater of:

- your relevant UK earnings chargeable to UK income tax for that tax year; or
- the basic amount of £3,600 where relief at source is provided.

The total amount of tax relief you can benefit from is also limited by the Annual Allowance.

Enjoying UK pension benefits abroad

Unfortunately pension scheme and annuity providers do not typically pay your pension benefits into an overseas account. So if you need to transfer the money from a UK bank account you will need to think about the impact of any transfer fees and exchange rate variations on the money you receive. When and how any benefits are exchange, may make a big difference to how much you will get.

Building up a UK State Pension from abroad

You may be able to build up a UK State Pension if you pay into the social security system of:

- a country in the European Economic Area; (Keep an eye on BREXIT)
- Switzerland;
- a country that has a social security agreement with the UK.

You may also be able to claim a State Pension from the country you are living in, if you are paying into its state pension scheme.

Receiving a UK State Pension abroad

You are allowed to live in another country and receive the UK State Pension. However you will only receive pension increases each year if you live in:

- the UK for 6 months or more each year;
- the European Economic Area (EEA);
- Switzerland;
- A country that has a social security agreement with the UK that allows for increases.

If you live outside these areas, you won't get yearly increases. However, if you return to live permanently in the UK, your State Pension will be increased each year.

If you move overseas after you have started to receive your State Pension you should inform the pension service when you are going to leave.

To find out more about State Pensions and benefits if you live or have lived overseas, and to claim your benefits, go to www.gov.uk/international-pension-centre.

*****

Chapter 12

Pensions for the Self-Employed

If you're self-employed, saving into a pension can be a more difficult habit to develop than it is for people in employment. There is no-one to choose a pension scheme for you, no employer contributions and irregular income patterns which can all make saving difficult. But preparing for retirement is crucial for you too.

The State Pension

If you're self-employed you're entitled to the State Pension in the same way as anyone else. As we have discussed, from April 2016 there is a new flat rate State Pension which is based entirely on your National Insurance (NI) record. There is a minimum requirement of 35 years NI contributions.

For the current tax year (2019/2020) the new State Pension is £168.60 per week. However, if you worked for someone else rather than yourself in the past, you might have built up entitlement to additional State Pension under the old system and get more than this. To find out how much you have built up under the State Pension get a State Pension statement on the Gov.uk website

But on its own, the State Pension is unlikely to provide you with enough income to maintain the standard of living you might like. So it's crucial you plan how to provide yourself with the rest of the retirement income you'll need.

How best to save for retirement

There are around 4.5 million people in the UK who are self-employed and this number is increasing. Yet the number of self-employed people saving into a pension has halved. One big attraction of being self-employed is you don't have a boss. But, in terms of pensions, this is a disadvantage.

By 2018 all employers will have had to provide a workplace pension scheme for their employees and pay into it, boosting the amount their employees are saving towards retirement. If you're self-employed, you won't have an employer adding money to your pension in this way. But there are still some tax breaks you shouldn't miss out on. For example, you'll get tax relief on your contributions, usually up to £40,000 a year. This means if you're a basic-rate taxpayer, for every £100 you pay into your pension, the government will add an extra £25. If you are a higher rate taxpayer you can claim back a further £25 for every £100 you pay in through your tax return.

Make the most of your pension pot

The earlier you start saving into a pension, the better. It gives you more time to contribute to your savings before retirement, more time to benefit from tax relief, and more time for your savings to grow. Starting early could more than double your pension pot:

See overleaf.

*Assuming savings grew at 5% a year and charges were 0.75% a year

You pay	Government pays	Start saving at age	Pension pot at 65
£100	£25	30	£70,000
£100	£25	40	£46,000
£100	£25	50	£25,000*

Self-employed: what kind of pension should I use?

Most self-employed people use a personal pension for their pension savings. With a personal pension you choose where you want your contributions to be invested from a range of funds offered by the provider. The provider will claim tax relief at the basic rate of tax on your behalf and add it to your pension savings. How much you get back depends on how much is paid in, how well your savings perform, and the level of charges you pay.

There are three types of personal pension which we have discussed in the previous chapters: ordinary personal pensions which are offered by most large providers; stakeholder pensions where the maximum charge is capped at 1.5% and you can stop and start premiums without penalty and self-invested personal pensions which have a wider range of investment options, but usually higher charges.

Alternatively, self-employed people can also use NEST (National Employment Savings Trust) which is the workplace pension scheme created by government for auto enrolment. It's run as a trust by the NEST Corporation which means there are no shareholders or owners and it's run for the benefit of its members. Although NEST is primarily for people who are employed, they also allow some self-employed people to save with them.

If you are not sure which scheme to save with it would be worth consulting a regulated financial adviser who will make a recommendation based on your specific needs and circumstances. The benefit of taking regulated financial advice is you're protected if the product you buy turns out to be unsuitable or in the unlikely event the provider goes bust. But mostly the benefit is a financial adviser can search the whole market for you and make a recommendation personal to you.

What is the annual allowance?

As we have seen, you can save as much as you like towards your pension each year, but there's a limit on the amount that will get tax relief.

The maximum amount of pension savings benefiting from tax relief each year is called the annual allowance. The annual allowance for 2018-2019 is £40,000. If you go over £40,000, you won't get tax relief on further pension savings. You can usually carry forward unused annual allowance from the previous three years.

For more details concerning pensions for the self employed you should go to The Pensions Advice Service on pensionsadvisoryservice.org.uk

Rules for Doctors and Dentists

GP's or dentists working in a practice are counted as self-employed for tax purposes. However, they are eligible to contribute to an occupational pension scheme-the National Health Service Pension Scheme, which is defined in the National Health Service Pension Scheme Regulations 2008. You should go to www. nhspa.gov.uk for more information.

At the same time GP's and dentists can contribute to a personal pension scheme.

If a person belongs to the NHS scheme they can make Additional Voluntary Contributions (AVC's) as long as total contributions don't exceed the normal limit applying to an employers scheme. AVC's can be made either to the NHS scheme or to a free-standing AVC scheme.

*****

Chapter 13

Pensions and Benefits for Dependants

___

State pensions

If you die before your spouse or civil partner has reached state pension age there may be some entitlement to state bereavement benefits if you have built up the appropriate NI contributions in the years prior to your death. The following may be available:

- Bereavement payment. This is a tax-free lump sum of £2500 (Standard rate for deaths occurring after 6th April 2017) or £3,500 higher rate.

- Widowed Parent's Allowance. This is a taxable income (£119.90 a week (2019/20) plus half of any additional state pension (S2P) you had built up. The payment continues until the youngest child ceases to be dependant or until your widow, widower or civil partner, enters a new marriage or civil partnership or starts to live with someone as if they were married or registered. Your spouse or civil partner might also be able to claim Child tax credit (CTC, a means tested state benefit available to households with children).

- Bereavement allowance. This is a regular taxable payment payable to spouses and civil partners over age 45 without any dependant children. The amount increases with their age. This is payable for a maximum of 52 weeks and will cease if a spouse or civil partner remarries.

Death after retirement

If you die after you and your spouse/civil partner have both reached State Pension age help is given through the State pension system. Your spouse or partner, if they do not receive a full basic pension in their own right, may be able to make up the pension to the full single person's rate, currently £129.20 per week (2019/20) by using your contribution record. In addition, they can inherit half of any additional State Pension you had built up.

To find out more about bereavement benefits contact your local jobcentre plus, if you are of working age at www.direct.gov.uk. Advice on a full range of bereavement benefits for those who are retired can also be obtained here.

Occupational and personal schemes

Occupational and personal schemes may also offer pensions and lump sum pay-outs for your survivors when you die. Schemes can pay pensions to your dependants (but not anyone who was not dependant or co-dependant on you) whether you die before or after you started your pension. This means your husband, wife, civil partner, children under the age of 23 or, if older, dependant on you because of physical or mental impairment.

Also, anyone else financially dependant on you can benefit. Under the tax rules, all the dependants pensions added together must not come to more than the retirement pension you would have been entitled to, but otherwise there is no limit on the amount of any one pension, although individual scheme rules may set some limits.

Dependant's pensions from occupational salary-related schemes

Subject to tax rules governing such schemes, a scheme can set its own rules about how much pension it will provide for dependants. Typically, a scheme will provide a pension for a widow, widower, civil partner or unmarried partner on:

- death before you have started your pension
- death after you have started your pension.
- This will typically be half or two thirds of the pension that you were entitled to at the time of your death. The pension must be increased in line with inflation. If you have been contracted out through a salary related pension scheme before April 1977, the scheme must pay a guaranteed minimum pension (GMP) to the person entitled equal to half the GMP's you had built up.

Lump sum death benefits

The options available to your beneficiaries after you die will depend on how you choose to take your pension and at what age you die. In the event of your death whilst in drawdown your beneficiaries will have the following options under the current rules:

- **Take the pension as a lump sum** Any beneficiary can inherit some or all of your remaining fund. They can do what they like with it. This payment will be tax free if you die before reaching age 75, or taxed at the beneficiary's marginal rate of income tax if after.

- **Continue with drawdown** A dependant or nominated beneficiary can continue to receive your fund as drawdown. Income from which will be tax free if you die before reaching age 75, or taxed at the beneficiary's marginal rate of income tax if after.
- **Convert the drawdown fund to a lifetime annuity** A dependant or nominated beneficiary can use your remaining drawdown fund to purchase a lifetime annuity. The income will be tax free if you die before reaching age 75, or taxed at the beneficiary's marginal rate of income tax if after.

Pensions are typically held in trust outside your estate and so in most cases are free of inheritance tax (IHT). Death benefits set up more than two years after death may lose their tax-free status. If you make a pension contribution or reduce the income you are drawing from your drawdown plan while in ill health or within two years of death the funds may still be liable to IHT. Tax charges may also apply if you exceed the lifetime allowance and die before age 75.

This information is based on 6 April 2019 pension rules and is subject to change. Tax rules & benefits can change and their value will depend on your personal circumstances.

*****

Chapter 14

Protecting Pensions

It is not surprising that people get very disillusioned and nervous when it comes to pensions. Since the 1980's there have been a number of scandals involving blatant theft of pensions and also incidences of miss-selling.

During the 1950's, one of Britain's biggest insurance companies, Equitable life, offered pensions which were supposed to guarantee a fixed level of income at retirement. However, by the 1990's these guarantees became too expensive and the company could not fulfill their promises. Equitable life faced many legal challenges and stopped taking on any new business. Many pensioners found themselves with poor returns and it is only recently that the government looking at compensating the victims.

In addition to theft and bad management the usual raft of 'financial advisors' miss-sold personal pensions, taking advantage particularly of the changes in the 1980's and peoples confusion. Although many people received compensation, many others did not and a lot of distress was caused to a lot of people.

To add to the above a lot of companies became insolvent and there was too little in the pension funds to fulfill pension promises. In the early days (early 2000's) there was a spate of these insolvencies and lots of people lost their pension or received less than they had planned for. The government set up several schemes to help such people and a compensation scheme was set up to assist.

The main risk to pension funds lies with occupational schemes. Although people need to be aware of changes to the state pension scheme it is safe in so far as the state is unlikely to become insolvent and unable to pay. For sure people need to keep abreast of legislation and changes to state pensions but in essence the amount promised will remain safe.

Occupational schemes

One of the main risks to occupational pensions is that the employer might embezzle the funds. This should be difficult given the role of the pension trustees, which will be outlined below, but it is always possible. There is also the risk that the scheme cannot pay the amount promised. This can be to do with stock market fluctuations, or, as we have all painfully seen in the last few years, a deep recession which affects people and pensions globally.

Another problem that may arise is that of schemes with defined benefits, final salary schemes, changing their rules and replacing defined benefits with less generous schemes.

Protecting pensions

Occupational schemes are usually either statutory schemes or are set up under a trust. A statutory scheme is as the name implies. It is set up under an Act of Parliament and is the usual arrangement for most public sector schemes such as police, NHS, teachers and so on. Private sector schemes are usually always set up under a trust. This ensures that the scheme is kept at arms length from the employer and business, and can't go down with the sinking ship. (Many lessons have been learned post-Mirror Group and Robert Maxwell).

With a trust you will have three main elements:

- The sponsor, who will be the employer, who will initially decide on the rules of the scheme along with the benefits
- the beneficiaries, who are scheme members and any beneficiaries who might benefit if, say, a scheme member passes away
- Very importantly, the trustees who are tasked with looking after the pension fund and making sure that it is administered in accordance with the scheme rules.

The trustees are responsible for the running of the scheme but can also employ outside help, specialist help and can employ someone to administrate the scheme. They are supported in this role by the Pensions Regulator, which is the official body that regulates all worked based schemes (occupational schemes and also those personal pensions and stakeholder schemes organized through the workplace). The Pensions Regulator promotes good practice, monitors risk, investigates schemes and responds to complaints from scheme members. The Pensions Regulator has many powers, as would be expected, and can prosecute those who it thinks guilty of wrongdoing.

There is a Fraud Compensation Fund which can pay out where an occupational pension schemes assets have been embezzled or reduced because of dishonest activity. The fund is financed by a levy on all occupational pension schemes.

Other schemes

Normally, if there is a shortfall when a pension scheme is wound up, the employer would be expected to make up any shortfall. However, clearly this is not possible if the employer is insolvent and there is no money to put into a scheme. Between 1997 and 2005 some 85,000 people lost some or all of their promised pensions because of insolvency.

Because of this several schemes were set up to provide protection:

- Financial Assistance Scheme (FAS). This scheme was set up and funded by the government to provide help for those pensions scheme members in greatest need where their pension scheme started to wind up between 1st January 1997 to 5th April 2005. This is administered by the Pensions Regulator.
- Pension Protection Fund (PPF). This scheme took over from the above to provide compensation where a scheme winds up on or after 6th April 2005 with too little in the fund or an insolvent employer. In general, compensation ensures that existing pensioners carry on getting the full amount of their pension and that other scheme members get 90% of their promised pension up to a maximum limit (£39,006.18 at 65 in 2018). The PPF is financed by a levy on occupational pension schemes.

For full details of the Pension protection fund you should go to www.pensionprotectionfund.org.uk.

Protection of personal pensions

Nearly all personal pensions come under the umbrella of the Financial Conduct Authority (FCA). In the United Kingdom, it is illegal to offer personal pensions without being authorized by the FCA. All pension providers authorized by then FCA have to go through a lot of hoops to demonstrate that they are responsible providers. The FCA oversees the activities of the Financial Services Compensation Scheme. If a firm providing personal pensions becomes insolvent the FSCS will step in and provide compensation instead. Compensation is capped at a maximum amount, which varies according to the way that your money has been invested. Currently the maximum is £85,000 for deposits, £50,000 for investments and for long term insurance (personal pensions, life insurance and annuities 90% of the claim with no upper limit).

State pensions

In the first instance you would deal with HMRC, regarding payment of national insurance, and also the Pension Service regarding pension forecasts. You can find details about how to complain from HMRC website www.hmrc.gov.uk. If you have complained to the director of a particular office and you are not happy you can take your complaint to the Adjudicators Office (www.adjudicatorsoffice.gov.uk).

This is an independent body that can deal with complaints about mistakes and delays, misleading advice and any other issue. In the same way you should contact the Pensions Service department dealing with pension forecasts if you have a problem in this area. If the problem carries on without resolution you can contact the Pensions Service Chief Executive.

Occupational schemes

You should initially contact the pension administrator for your scheme. If the problem is not resolved at this early stage then you should say that you want to use the formal complaints procedure, which all occupational schemes must have and must provide you with details of. If you receive no satisfaction with this process then you should contact The Pensions Advisory Service (TPAS) www.pensionsadvisoryservice.org.uk.

TPAS is an independent mediation service which will help all parties reach agreement. If this doesn't work then you can go one step further and take your complaint to the Pensions Ombudsman. You must go through TPAS before the Ombudsman will consider your complaint.

Personal pensions

You should complain first to the pensions provider. As mentioned, all firms authorized by the FCA must have a formal complaints procedure. Provided that you go down this route, and you are still unhappy, then you can complain to the Financial Ombudsman Service (FOS) www.financial-ombudsman.org.uk. It will investigate your complaint and can make orders which are binding on the firm. Where appropriate the FOS can make the firm pay you up to £100,000 to put the matter right.

*****

Chapter 15

Pensions-Options for Retirement and Tax Implications for Private Pensions

---

Retirement options and taxation of pensions

As you will know by now, changes introduced from April 2015 give you freedom over how you can access your pension savings if you're 55 or over and have a pension based on how much has been paid into your pot (such as a defined contribution, money purchase or cash balance scheme).

Options for using your pension pot

Depending on your age and personal circumstances some or all of the options outlined below could be suitable for you. Your main options, which we will discuss in greater detail are:

1. Keep your pension savings where they are and take them later on in life.
2. Use your pension pot to get a guaranteed income for life – called a Lifetime annuity. The income is taxable, but you can choose to take up to 25% of your pot as a one-off tax-free lump sum at the outset.
3. Use your pension pot to provide a Flexible retirement income, take 25% of your pension pot (or 25% of the amount you allocate for this option) as a tax-free lump sum, then use the rest to provide a regular taxable income.

4. Take a number of lump sums – the first 25% of each cash withdrawal from your pot will be tax-free. The rest will be taxed.
5. Take your pension pot in one go – the first 25% will be tax-free and the rest is taxable.
6. Mix your options – choose any combination of the above, using different parts of your pot or separate pots.

We will now look at each of these six options, and the implications, in turn.

1. Keep your pension savings where they are

With this option, your pot continues to grow tax-free until you need it – potentially providing more income once you start taking money out. You (and your employer) can continue making contributions however there are restrictions on how much you can save each year and over a lifetime and still receive tax relief.

In most cases you can get tax relief on pension contributions, including any employer contributions, on the lower of 100% of your earnings or up to £40,000 each year (2019-20 tax year) until age 75. However, if you are a high earner the limit on how much tax-free money you can build up in your pension in any one year depends on your 'adjusted income'. If you don't pay Income Tax, you can still get tax relief on up to £3,600 of pension savings each year until age 75.

However, you will need to check with your pension scheme or provider whether there are any restrictions or charges for changing your retirement date, and the process and deadline for telling them. You need to know whether there are any costs for leaving your pot where it is – some providers charge an administration fee for continuing to manage your pension. Check that you won't lose any valuable income guarantees – for example, a guaranteed annuity rate – if you delay your retirement date.

One other important point is that the money you have saved into your pension pot could continue to grow, but it could also go down in value, as with any investment. Remember to review where your pot is invested as you get closer to the time you want to retire and arrange to move it to less risky funds if necessary.

If you want your pot to remain invested after the age of 75, you'll need to check that your pension scheme or provider will allow this. If not, you may need to transfer to another scheme or provider who will. Not all pension schemes and providers will allow you to delay. If you want to delay but don't have this option, shop around before moving your pension.

On death, any unused pension pots normally fall outside your estate for Inheritance Tax purposes and can be passed on to any nominated beneficiary. In both cases the money continues to grow tax-free while still invested.

If you die before age 75: Provided the beneficiary takes the money within two years of the provider being notified of the pension holder's death, they can take it as a tax-free lump sum or as tax-free income. If they take it later (whether as a lump sum or income) it will be added to their other income and taxed at the appropriate Income Tax rate.

If you die age 75 or over: When the money is taken out (lump sum or income) it will be added to the beneficiary's income and taxed at the appropriate Income Tax rate. However, if the beneficiary is not an individual but is, for example, a company or trust, any lump sum will be taxed at 45%.

2. Use your pension pot to get a guaranteed income for life

A guaranteed income for life – known as a lifetime annuity – provides you with a guarantee that the money will last as long as you live. Guaranteed lifetime income products include: basic lifetime annuities; Investment-linked annuities.

The options

You can choose to take up to 25% (a quarter) of your pot as a one-off tax-free lump sum at the outset. You use the rest to buy a guaranteed lifetime income – a lifetime annuity – from your provider or another insurance company. You must buy within six months of taking your tax-free lump sum. As a rule of thumb, the older you are when you take out a guaranteed lifetime income product, the higher the income you'll get. You can choose to receive your income monthly, quarterly, half-yearly or yearly, depending on the scheme or provider. This type of income is taxable.

Basic lifetime annuities

Basic lifetime annuities offer a range of income options designed to match different personal circumstances. You need to decide whether you want:

- one that provides a guaranteed income for you only and stops when you die –a single life annuity, or one that also provides an income for life for a dependant or other nominated beneficiary after you die – a joint life annuity (normally provides a lower regular income as it's designed to pay out for longer)

- payments to continue to a nominated beneficiary for a set number of years (for example 10 years) from the time the guaranteed income starts, in case you die unexpectedly early – called a guarantee period (can be combined with a single or joint life annuity). For example, if you opt for a guarantee period of 10 years and die after two years, the payments to a nominated beneficiary would continue for eight years.

- payments fixed at the same amount throughout your life – a level annuity, or payments to be lower than a level annuity to start with but rise over time by set amounts – an escalating annuity – or in line with inflation – an inflation-linked annuity.

- value protection – less commonly used and likely to reduce the amount of income you receive, but designed to pay your nominated beneficiary the value of the pot used to buy the guaranteed lifetime income less income already paid out when you die.

Investment-linked annuities

If you're willing to take more risk in return for a potentially higher income, you could opt for an income that is investment-linked (known as an investment-linked annuity). The income you receive rises and falls in line with the value of investments that you choose when you purchase your product. So while it could pay more over the longer term than a basic annuity, your income could also fall.

Many investment-linked annuities guarantee a minimum income if the fund's performance is weak. With investment-linked annuities you can also have a dependant's pension, guarantee periods, value protection and higher rates if you have a short life expectancy due to poor health or lifestyle. Some investment-linked annuities allow you to change your investment options or allow you to take lower payments later.

Although you can't change your guaranteed income back into a pension pot, the government has announced changes due to come into force in early 2017 that may allow you to sell your product for a cash lump sum on which you may have to pay Income Tax. How much tax you pay would depend on the value of your product, and your overall income in that year.

Think carefully about whether you need to provide an income for your partner or another dependant on your death. Consider whether you should take a product which provides an increasing income. Inflation (the general rise in price of goods and services over time) can significantly reduce your standard of living over time. Investment-linked annuities offer the chance of a higher income – but only by taking extra risk. Your income could reduce if the fund doesn't perform as expected. If you're considering this option look at what your provider can offer then get financial advice.

If you buy guaranteed income with money from a pension pot you've already used for another income option (e.g. to provide a flexible retirement income) you can't take a further tax-free lump sum – even if you chose not to take a tax-free lump sum with the other option. Not all pension schemes and providers offer guaranteed lifetime income products. Some may only offer one type, or offer to buy one on your behalf.

Whatever the case, shop around before deciding who to go with – you're likely to get a better income than sticking with your current provider.

Tax

You will have to pay tax on the income you receive, in the same way you pay tax on your salary. How much you pay depends on your total income and the Income Tax rate that applies to you. Your provider will take tax off your income before you receive it

Because they won't know your overall income they will use an emergency tax code to start with. This means you may pay too much tax initially and have to claim the money back – or you may owe more tax if you have other sources of income. If the value of all of your pension savings is above £1,055,000m (2019-20 tax year) and these savings haven't already been assessed against the Lifetime allowance, further tax charges may apply when you access your pension pot.

Tax relief on future pension savings

After buying a guaranteed income product you can in most cases continue to get tax relief on pension savings of up to the Annual allowance of £40,000 (2019-20). However, if you buy a lifetime annuity which could decrease such as an investment-linked annuity, the maximum future defined contribution pension savings that can be made in a year that qualifies for tax relief is limited to the lower of £10,000 (the Money purchase annual allowance) or 100% of your earnings. If you want to carry on saving into a pension this option may not be suitable.

On death, if you have a single life guaranteed income product and no other features, your pension stops when you die. Otherwise, the tax rules vary depending on your age as shown below.

If you die before age 75: Income from a joint guaranteed income product will be paid to your dependant or other nominated beneficiary tax-free for the rest of their life. If you die within a guarantee period the remaining payments will pass tax-free to your nominated beneficiary then stop when the guarantee period ends. Any lump sum payment due from a value protected guaranteed lifetime income product will be paid tax-free. It will also normally fall outside your estate for Inheritance Tax purposes.

If you die age 75 or over: Income from a joint guaranteed income product or a continuing guarantee period will be added to the beneficiary's overall income and taxed at the appropriate Income Tax rate. Joint payments will stop when your dependant or other beneficiary dies and any guarantee period payments stop when the guarantee period ends. Any lump sum due from a value protected guaranteed income product will be added to the beneficiary's overall income and taxed at the appropriate Income Tax rate. Lump sums due from a value protected guaranteed income product normally fall outside your estate for Inheritance Tax purpose.

3. Use your pension pot to provide a flexible retirement income

You can move all or some of your pension pot into an investment specifically designed to provide an income for your retirement . The income isn't guaranteed but you have flexibility to make changes. This is sometimes called 'Flexi-access drawdown'.

You can choose to take up to 25% (a quarter) of your pension pot as a tax-free lump sum. You then move the rest within six months into one or more funds (or other assets) that allow you to take income at times to suit you – e.g. monthly, quarterly, yearly or irregular withdrawals. Most people use it to take a regular income. If you don't move the rest of your money within the six months, you'll be charged tax (normally 55% of the un-transferred fund value). Once you've taken your tax-free lump sum, you can start taking the income right away, or wait until a later date. The income is taxable.

Unlike with a guaranteed income for life (a lifetime annuity), the retirement income you receive from a flexible retirement income product is not guaranteed to last as long as you live, so you should think carefully about how much you withdraw.

Deciding how much income you can afford to take needs careful planning – it depends on how much money you put in from your pension pot, the performance of the funds, what other sources of income you have, and whether you want to provide for a dependant or someone else after you die. It also depends on how long you will live. Your retirement income could fall or even run out if you take too much too soon and start eating into the money you originally invested to produce the income – especially if stock markets fall. Investment choice is key – you will need to review where your money is invested regularly to ensure it continues to meet your long-term retirement income needs. Investments can fall as well as rise – you'll need to know how you'll cope if your income suddenly drops.

Not all pension schemes and providers offer flexible retirement income products. If yours doesn't, you can transfer your pension pot to another provider who does but again there may be a fee to do so. Different providers will offer different features and charging structures on their products – and the choice is likely to increase.

You pay tax on the income withdrawals (outside the tax-free cash allowance). How much tax you pay depends on your total income and the Income Tax rate that applies to you. Your provider will take tax off your income payments in advance. Because they won't know your overall income they will use an emergency tax code to start with which means you may initially pay too much tax – and have to claim the money back – or you may owe more tax if you have other sources of income. If you have other income, you'll need to plan carefully how much flexible retirement income to take, to avoid pushing yourself into a higher tax bracket. If the value of all of your pension savings is above £1m (2016-17 tax year) and these savings haven't already been assessed against the Lifetime allowance, further tax charges may apply when you access your pension pot.

Tax relief on future pension savings

Once you have taken any money from your flexible retirement income product, the maximum future defined contribution pension savings that can be made in a year that qualifies for tax relief is limited to the lower of £4,000 (the Money purchase annual allowance – down from the usual £40,000 Annual allowance in 2019-20) or 100% of your earnings. If you want to carry on building up your pension pot, this may influence when you start taking your flexible retirement income. The tax relief you get for future pension savings is not affected if you take the tax-free lump sum but no income.

On death, any remaining flexible retirement income funds when you die normally fall outside your estate for Inheritance Tax purposes.

If you die before age 75: Anything remaining in your fund passed to a nominated beneficiary within two years of notifying the provider of the pension holder's death will be tax-free whether they take it as a lump sum or as income. If it is over two years any money paid will be added to the beneficiary's income and taxed at their appropriate rate.

If you die age 75 or above: Anything remaining in your fund that you pass on – either as a lump sum or income – will be taxed at the beneficiary's appropriate Income Tax rate.

4. Take your pension pot as a number of lump sums

You can leave your money in your pension pot and take lump sums from it when you need it, until your money runs out or you choose another option.

You take cash from your pension pot as and when you need it and leave the rest invested where it can continue to grow tax-free. For each cash withdrawal the first 25% (quarter) will be tax-free and the rest is taxable. There may be charges each time you make a cash withdrawal and/or limits on how many withdrawals you can make each year. Unlike with the flexible retirement income option your pot isn't re-invested into new funds specifically chosen to pay you a regular income.

This option won't provide a regular income for you, or for any dependant after you die. Your pension pot reduces with each cash withdrawal. The earlier you start taking money out the greater the risk that your money could run out – or what's left won't grow sufficiently to generate the income you need to last you into old age.

Remember, as we saw in chapter 2, the buying power of cash reduces because of rising prices over time (inflation) – using cash sums to fund your long-term retirement isn't advisable. If you plan to use cash withdrawals to make a one-off purchase or to pay down debts, you must also be sure that you have enough left to live on for the rest of your life.

In addition, it is worth noting that this option won't provide a regular retirement income for you or for any dependants after you die.

Not all pension providers or schemes offer the ability to withdraw your pension pot as a number of lump sums. Shop around if you want this option but can't get it with your current provider, as charges and restrictions will vary. You may not be able to use this option if you have primary protection or enhanced protection, and protected rights to a tax-free lump sum of more than £375,000 (protections that relate to the LIfetime Allowance).

Tax

Three-quarters (75%) of each cash withdrawal counts as taxable income. This could increase your tax rate when added to your other income. How much tax you pay depends on your total income and the Income Tax rate that applies to you. Your pension scheme or provider will pay the cash and take off tax in advance. Because they won't know your overall income they will use an emergency tax code to start with. This means you may pay too much tax and have to claim the money back – or you may owe more tax if you have other sources of income. If the value of all of your pension savings is above £1,055,000m and these savings haven't already been assessed against the Lifetime allowance (2019-20 tax year), further tax charges may apply when you access your pension pot. Once you reach age 75, if you have less remaining Lifetime allowance available than the amount you want to withdraw, the amount you will get tax-free will be limited to 25% (a quarter) of your remaining Lifetime allowance, rather than 25% of the amount you are taking out.

Tax relief on future pension savings

Once you have taken a lump sum, the maximum future defined contribution pension savings that can be made in a year that qualifies for tax relief is limited to the lower of £4,000 (the Money purchase annual allowance – down from the £40,000 Annual allowance for most people in 2019-20) or 100% of your earnings. If you want to carry on saving into a pension, this option may not be suitable.

On death any untouched part of your pension pot normally falls outside your estate for Inheritance Tax purposes.

If you die before age 75: Any untouched part of your pension pot will pass tax-free to your nominated beneficiary provided the money is claimed within 2 years of notifying the provider of the pension holder's death. If it is over 2 years the money will be added to the beneficiary's other income and taxed at the appropriate rate.

If you die age 75 or over: Any untouched part of your pension pot that you pass on - either as a lump sum or income - will be added to the beneficiary's overall income and taxed at the appropriate Income Tax rate.

5. Take your pension pot in one go

You no longer have to convert your pension pot into an income if you don't want to. You can take out all of your pension savings in one go if you wish. Cashing in your pension pot will not give you a secure retirement income. Basically, you close your pension pot and withdraw it all as cash. The first 25% (quarter) will be tax-free and the rest will be taxable.

This option won't provide a regular income for you – or for your spouse, civil partner or other dependant after you die. Three-quarters (75%) of the amount you withdraw is taxable income, so there's a strong chance your tax rate would go up when the money is added to your other income. If you choose this option you can't change your mind – so you need to be certain that it's right for you. For many or most people it will be more tax efficient to consider one or more of the other options. If you plan to use the cash to clear debts, buy a holiday, or indulge in a big-ticket item you need to think carefully before committing to this option.

Doing so will reduce the money you will have to live on in retirement, and you could end up with a large tax bill. In addition, you may not be able to use this option if you have primary protection or enhanced protection, and protected rights to a tax-free lump sum of more than £375,000 (protections that relate to the LIfetime Allowance). It is best to talk to your scheme if you have one or more of these kinds of protection and find out what your options are. There may be charges for cashing in your whole pot. Check with your scheme or provider. Not all pension schemes and providers offer cash withdrawal – shop around then get financial advice if you still want this option after considering its risks, as charges may vary.

Tax relief on future pension savings

Once you have cashed in your pension pot, the maximum future defined contribution pension savings that can be made in a year that qualifies for tax relief is limited to the lower of £4,000 (the Money purchase annual allowance – down from the usual £40,000 Annual allowance which will apply for most people in 2019-20) or 100% of your earnings.

On death, whatever age you die, any money remaining or investments bought with cash taken out of your pension pot will count as part of your estate for Inheritance Tax. By contrast, any part of your pot that was untouched would not normally be liable.

6. Mixing your options

You don't have to choose one option – you can mix and match as you like over time or over your total pension pot, whichever suits your needs. You can also keep saving into a pension if you wish, and get tax relief up to age 75. Which option or combination is right for you will depend on:

- when you stop or reduce your work
- your income objectives and attitude to risk
- your age and health
- the size of your pension pot and other savings

- any pension or other savings of your spouse or partner, if relevant
- the possible effect on your entitlement to State benefits
- whether you have financial dependants
- whether your circumstances are likely to change in the future.

Tax-free lump sums when mixing options

Note that depending on how you access money from your pension pot you may only get one chance to take your tax-free amount. This can be anything up to 25% (a quarter) of the amount you access and must be taken at that time. For example, if you use your whole pension pot to provide a flexible retirement income, you use up your rights to take a tax-free sum at the time you transfer the funds. So whether you choose to take 25% tax-free, or less – or no tax-free sum at all – you can't take a tax-free lump sum later if, for example, you decide to use part of your flexible retirement income fund to buy a guaranteed income for life (an annuity). However, if you only used part of your pot to buy a flexible retirement income and later wanted to use some or all of the remaining part of your pension pot to buy a regular income for life (a lifetime annuity), you could take up to 25% of that money as tax-free cash.

On death, the same rules apply for passing on your remaining pension as already set out for each option.

For more advice on pensions and tax go to www.pensionsadvisoryservice.org.uk

Chapter 16

Reaching Retirement Age

We have discussed many of the issues in this section in previous chapters. Nevertheless it is worth reiterating them as when you reach retirement age you will want to know the practical issues such as how do you claim your pension.

On reaching retirement age, it will be necessary to ensure that all paperwork relating to pension contributions is in order. There are a number of rules that should be observed in order to ensure that any pension due is paid:

- keep all documents relating to pension rights
- start organising any pension due before retirement, this will ensure that any problems are overcome well before retirement

It is very important that communication is kept with all pension providers, and that they have accurate up-to-date records of a person's whereabouts. Each time addresses are changed this should be communicated to all pension providers. If it is impossible to track down an old employer from whom a pension is due, the Pension Schemes Registry can help. The Pensions Regulator is responsible for the Pension Schemes Registry. This was set up in 1990, by the government to help people trace so-called 'lost pensions'. If help is needed this can be obtained by filling in a form which can be accessed on the website of the pensions regulator www.pensionsregulator.gov.uk

How to claim state pension

A letter will be sent to all retiree's about four months before retirement date. This will come from the pension service and will detail how much pension is due. The pension is not paid automatically, it has to be claimed. This can be done by phoning the Pensions Claim Line number included with the letter, or by filling in a claim form BR1. If the person is a married man and the wife is claiming based on the husbands contributions, then form BF225 should be filled in. If the pension is to be deferred it is advisable to contact the Pensions Service in writing as soon as possible at www. pensionsadvisoryservice.org.uk. A late pension claim can be backdated up to twelve months. If a man is claiming for a pension for his wife based on his contributions this can only be backdated six-months.

How the pension is paid

Pensions are paid by the DWP pension direct to a bank account or Post Office Card Account. To find out more about the payment of pensions contact the DWP www.gov.uk/government/organisations/department-for-work-pensions.

Leaving the country

If a person goes abroad for less than six months, they can carry on receiving pension in the normal way. If the trip is for longer then the Pension Service should be contacted and one of the following arrangements can be made to pay a pension: Have it paid into a personal bank account while away; arrange for it to be paid into a Post Office Card Account; arrange for the money to be paid abroad; If a person is living outside of the UK at the time of the annual pension increase they won't qualify for the increase unless they reside in a member country of the European Union or a country with which the UK has an agreement for increasing pensions. It is very important that you check what will happen to your state pension when you move abroad. The DWP International Pension Centre can help on 0191 218 7777, or access advice through their main website www.gov.uk/international-pension-centre.

Pensions from an occupational scheme

Although different schemes have different arrangements, there are similar rules for each scheme. About three months before a person reaches normal retirement age, they should contact the scheme. Either telephone or write enclosing all the details that they will need. The following questions should be asked:

- What pension is due?
- What is the lump-sum entitlement?
- How will the pension be reduced if a lump sum is taken?
- How will the pension be paid, will there be any choices as to frequency?
- Is there a widow's or widowers pension, and if so how will it affect the retirement pension?

- Are there any pensions for other dependants in the event of death?

If a person has been making Additional Voluntary Contributions, then a detailed breakdown of these will be needed.

A pension from a personal plan

In the same way as a pension from an occupational scheme, it is necessary to get in touch with the pension provider about 3-4 months before retirement date.

The main questions that should be asked are:

- How much is the pension fund worth?
- How much pension will the plan provider offer?
- Can an increase be arranged each year and if so how much is the increase?
- What is the maximum lump sum?
- Is there a widow's or widowers or other dependants pension?
- What are the other options if any?
- Can the purchase of an annuity be deferred without affecting the drawing of an income?

Pensions can only be paid by an insurance company or a friendly society so if the pension has been with any other form of provider then it has to be switched before it can be paid.

If there are protected-rights from a contracted out pension plan, these can be, may have to be, treated quite separately from the rest of a pension. Protected rights from a personal pension cannot be paid until a person has reached 60 years of age. A person must, by law, have an open market option enabling protected rights pension to be paid by another provider, if it is desired.

New regulations for pension providers

As we have discussed, at the end of February 2015, the government introduced new regulations that pension providers must abide by. Pension providers will have to give specific risk warnings to savers looking to take advantage of the 2015 reforms. Any regulated company that sells policies that offer a retirement income will have to tell customers about the tax implications of cashing in or investing their pension once the reforms are fully enacted from April 6th 2015. Pension companies must also highlight how a savers health could affect their retirement income. The providers must also provide advice on the effect on benefits and also warn of scams.

Advice schemes for pensions

To help people with the transition, the government has introduced a new advice service called Pension Wise. This will be administered through The Pensions Advisory Services (TPAS) and the Citizens Advice Bureau. This will be rolled out in march and April 2015. Pensioners with defined contribution pension savings-either a workplace money purchase plan or a personal pension plan-will be able to access the scheme. they should be 55 or over or near retirement and can register through the Pension Wise website www.pensionwise.gov.uk.

Customers will have to book an appointment to receive either phone based advice or one to one advice and the sessions will last up to 45 minutes. Guidance will include life expectancy, long term care needs, various pension products from annuities to drawdown and a tax calculator. The guidance is not the same as regulated financial advice, such as how to invest your money but is general guidance.

Beware of Scams

As we all know, there are scammers in every walk of life. This is how they make their living, usually having failed in legitimate enterprise. There have been warnings of increased scamming activity since the chancellor first announced the changes. Basically, scammers cold call people promising to unlock pensions before the April rules come into effect, luring people with promises of sky high returns on a number of ludicrous schemes, such as investment in property etc. In reality they are running off with your cash, leaving you with a sky high tax bill and no money. Scammers will also target people after the new rules come into effect promising high returns from investments.

The fundamental rule is: **avoid any cold callers** and those who promise anything at all. Avoid looking for free advice on the internet. **It is all bogus**. Manage your money yourself, after taking advice and guidance from the government scheme or through a financial advisor who is regulated by the Financial Conduct Authority. Always make sure that you are aware of the level of fees charged by financial advisors, as sometimes they can be quite high. Don't feel that you have to rush in if you are over 55. take your time and consider the options carefully.

The Pensions Dashboard

At the time of writing (2019) the government has announced that it is going ahead with the proposed pensions dashboard. This will be an extremely useful site which will enable workers and retirees to see all of their pensions details, both private and state pensions, on one website. For more information concerning the pensions dashboard and its progress go to pensionsdashboardproject.uk/saver/about-the-pensions-dashboard

Inheriting pensions on death

One important factor is the question of to whom do you leave your pension on death? Are your retirement policies updated in relation to who gets your pensions or is there a danger of the pension being passed on to the wrong person, such as an ex-husband or boyfriend or someone else who you would not like to see receive the pension?

The rise in the number of divorces, remarriages and couples co-habiting, plus a general apathy towards dealing with pensions when retirement is decades away, means many people could inadvertently be handing valuable benefits to former partners.

Pension schemes typically have an that allows members to name the person they want their benefits to go to when they die "expressions of wishes"

make sure that all of your details are updated to ensure that any benefits go to the person you want them to go to!

******

Useful Addresses

Association of Consulting Actuaries
First Floor (129)
40 Gracechurch Street
London EC3V OBT
Tel: 020 3102 6761
www.aca.org.uk

Association of Chartered Certified Accountants
The Adelphi
1-11 John Adam Street
London
WC2N 6AU
Tel: 0141 582 2000
Fax: 020 7059 5050
Email: info@accaglobal.com

Department for Work and Pensions (DWP)
www.gov.uk/government/organisations/department-for-work-pensions

Financial Conduct Authority (FCA)
12 Endeavour Square,
London,
E20 1JN
Consumer Helpline 0800 111 6768
www.fca.org.uk

Financial Services Compensation Scheme
10th Floor Beaufort House
15 St Botolph Street
London EC3A 7QU

0800 678 1100
www.fscs.org.uk

Financial Ombudsman Service
Exchange Tower
London E14 9SR
0800 0234 567
www.financialombudsman.org.uk

HMRC
For local tax enquiries look in phone book under HMRC
Or go to
www.hmrc.gov.uk

Institute of Chartered Accountants in England and Wales
Chartered Accountants Hall
1 Moorgate Place
London EC2R 6EA
020 7920 8100
www.icaew.co.uk

Institute of Chartered Accountants in Ireland
Chartered Accountants House
32-38 Linenhall Street
Belfast
Ireland
028 9043 5840
www.icai.ie

Institute of Chartered Accountants in Scotland
CA House
21 Haymarket Yards

Edinburgh EH12 5BH

0131 347 0313

www.icas.org.uk

Institute and faculty of Actuaries

1St Floor Park Central

40-41 Park End Street,

Oxford OX1 1JD

01865 268200

www.actuaries.org.uk

Institute of Financial Planning

www.financialplanning.org.uk

International Pension Centre

The Pension Service 11

Mail Handling Site A

Wolverhampton

WV98 1LW

0191 218 7777

Pensions Advisory Service

11 Belgrave Road

London SW1V 1RB

08000 113797

www.pensionsadvisoryservice.org.uk

Pensions Ombudsman

www. pensions-ombudsman.org.uk

Pensions Protection Fund

0330 123 2222

www.pensionprotectionfund.org.uk

Pension Tracing Service
www.pensiontracingservice.com
0800 123 170

Pension Service (The)
0800 731 7898 (Help making a claim)
www.gov.uk/contact-pension-service

Pension Wise
www.pensionwise.gov.uk

Society of Pension Professionals
Quantum House,
22-24 Red Lion Court,
London
EC4A 3EB
020 7353 1688
www.the-spp.uk.com

*****

Index

Additional state pension, 4, 44
Additional Voluntary Contributions, 119, 150
Advice schemes, 8, 151
Annual allowance, 60, 76, 137, 140, 143, 145
Auto Enrolment, 31, 77
Basic lifetime annuities, 8, 134
Basic state pensions, 35
Bereavement allowance, 121
Bereavement payment, 121

Capital gains Tax 69
Cash balance scheme, 84
Citizens Advice, 91, 151
Civil Partnerships Act 2004, 35
Class 1 contributions, 4, 39
Class 2 contributions, 39
Class 3 contributions, 39
Commercial property, 66, 68
Contracting out, 4, 45, 88
Contracting Out, 6, 87
Contributions into occupational schemes, 6, 85

Death after retirement, 7, 122
Deferring your state pension, 4, 47
Defined benefit, 57, 82
Defined contribution, 57
Dentists, 118
Department for Work and Pensions, 154
Department for Work and Pensions (DWP), 55
Dependants, 7, 62, 121
Doctors, 118

Fees, 5, 70
Filling gaps in your record, 4

Final salary schemes, 5, 82
Financial Assistance Scheme, 5, 128
Financial Conduct Authority, 6, 96, 129, 152
Financial Ombudsman Service (FOS), 130
Financial Services Authority, 61, 65, 154
Flexi-access drawdown, 139
Flexible retirement income,, 131
Fraud, 73, 127
Fraud Compensation Scheme., 73
Full state pension, 35

Group Pension Scheme, 77
Group personal pensions, 89
Guarantee credit, 40

How to claim state pension, 8, 148

Income drawdown, 61
Income needs in retirement, 3, 21
Increasing your state pension, 4, 45
Individual Savings Account (ISA, 33
Inflation, 3, 22, 136
Insurance company funds, 66
Investment trusts, 66
Investment-linked annuities, 8, 134, 135, 136
Investments, 4, 65, 139

Leaving the country, 8, 148
Lifetime allowance, 76, 137, 140, 143
Lifetime annuity, 131
Limits on your pension savings, 5, 75
Limits to benefits and contributions, 4, 60
Lump sum death benefits, 7, 123

Marriage (Same sex Couples Act) 2014, 35

Married women, 35, 44
Money purchase pension schemes, 83
Money purchase schemes, 5, 82, 83

National Health Service Pension Scheme, 118
National Health Service Superannuation Scheme, 118
National Insurance, 30, 45
National Insurance (NI) record, 115
National Insurance Credits, 4, 42
National Savings, 66

Obtaining a refund of contributions, 6, 101
Occupational pensions, 3, 30
Open Ended Investment Companies (OEICs, 68

Pension credits, 4, 40
Pension Protection Fund, 5, 72, 128
Pension Tracing Service, 5, 73, 157
Pensioners Income Series, 3, 12, 19
Pension-led funding, 70
Pensions Advisory Services (TPAS), 151
Pensions Regulator, 81, 82, 96, 97, 127, 128, 147
Personal pensions, 7, 130
Planning for the future, 3, 11
Protecting pensions, 29, 126

Qualifying to join an occupational scheme, 5, 77

Regional incomes, 3
Retirement due to ill-health, 5, 71
Retirement options, 7, 131

Same sex couples, 35
Scams, 152
Self-employed, 7, 32, 38, 39, 44, 117

Self-Employed, 7, 115
Self-invested Personal Pensions (SIPPs), 5, 65
SERPS, 29, 44
Single pensioners, 35
Small Self-Administered Schemes (Ssas), 5, 67
Sources of pension, 3, 11, 29
Stakeholder pension, 31, 96, 98
Stakeholder pensions, 6, 93, 95
Stakeholder schemes, 32
State Earnings Related Pension, 44
State second pension (S2P, 29
Stock Exchange, 68

Taking a pension, 4, 61, 71
Tax advantages of occupational schemes, 5, 76Tax free lump
    sum, 60
Tax relief, 6, 97, 137, 140, 143, 145
The annual allowance, 4, 60
The Financial Assistance Scheme, 5, 72
The lifetime allowance, 4, 57
The Pension Protection Fund, 5, 72
The Pension Tracing Service, 5, 73
The savings credit, 4, 40
The state pension, 29
Theft, 73
Traded endowment policies, 66
Transferring Pension Rights, 7, 103
Transsexual people, 36

Uncrystallised funds, 62
Widowed Parent's Allowance, 121
Winding up, 7
Winding up of occupational pension schemes, 7

Straightforward Guides

Buy online, using credit card or other forms of payment by going to www.straightfowardco.co.uk. A discount of 25% per title is offered with online purchases.

Law
A Straightforward Guide to:
Consumer Rights
Bankruptcy Insolvency and the Law
Employment Law
Private Tenants Rights
Family law
Small Claims in the County Court
Contract law
Intellectual Property and the law
Divorce and the law
Leaseholders Rights
The Process of Conveyancing
Knowing Your Rights and Using the Courts
Producing Your own Will
Housing Rights
Bailiffs and the Law
Litigants in Person
Probate and The Law
Company law
What to Expect When You Go to Court
Give me Your Money-Guide to Effective Debt Collection
The Rights of Disabled Children
The Rights of Disabled People

General titles

The Crime Writers casebook

Being a Detective

Letting Property for Profit

Buying, Selling and Renting property

Buying a Home in England and France

Bookkeeping and Accounts for Small Business

Understanding the Stock market

Creative Writing

Freelance Writing

Writing Your own Life Story

Writing performance Poetry

Writing Romantic Fiction

Speech Writing

Creating a Successful Commercial Website

The Straightforward Business Plan

The Straightforward C.V.

Successful Public Speaking

Handling Bereavement

Individual and Personal Finance

The Two-Minute Message

Go to: www.straightforwardco.co.uk

****